1973

be

THE REFERENCE SHELF   VOLUME 44 NUMBER 6

PRIORITIES
FOR SURVIVAL

EDITED BY
WILLIAM P. LINEBERRY

Editor, The Council on Foreign Relations

THE H. W. WILSON COMPANY
NEW YORK   1973

THE REFERENCE SHELF

The books in this series contain reprints of articles, excerpts from books, and addresses on current issues and social trends in the United States and other countries. There are six separately bound numbers in each volume, all of which are generally published in the same calendar year. One number is a collection of recent speeches; each of the others is devoted to a single subject and gives background information and discussion from various points of view, concluding with a comprehensive bibliography. Books in the series may be purchased individually or on subscription.

Library of Congress Cataloging in Publication Data

Lineberry, William P   comp.
    Priorities for survival.

    (The Reference shelf, v. 44, no. 6)
    SUMMARY: A compilation of articles concerned with man's prospects for survival in the ecological crisis, the virtues and vices of growth and technology, and the efforts made by governments and individuals to improve the environment.
    Bibliography: p.
    1. Environmental policy--United States--Addresses, essays, lectures. [1. Pollution. 2. Environmental policy. 3. Ecology] I. Title. II. Series.
HC110.E5L5   301.31'0973   72-11534
ISBN 0-8242-0469-7

PREFACE

"I believe," said William Faulkner in his speech accepting the Nobel Prize for Literature, "that man will not only endure—he will prevail." However lofty the sentiment, such buoyant optimism seems strangely out of place in our time, when a growing number of our leading analysts appear convinced that the cataclysm is imminent. With sudden power breakdowns threatening our larger cities; with man-made wastes poisoning our lakes, rivers, oceans, and the very air we breathe; with the earth's known supply of natural resources rapidly shrinking while humanity's own numbers go on steadily and unrestrainedly expanding—with such troubles besetting us even now, the future for our overcrowded, overexploited planet and all the creatures upon it looks bleak indeed. It may be true that men have been contending with the blight of pollution ever since they first left the forests to gather in cities. But the reek that scientists apparently detect in the atmosphere of our own time is, it would seem, all too fearfully akin to "cooked goose."

Can man survive the wonders of his own creation? Have all his mighty works been pointing to oblivion? The theme is being seriously argued by eminent and respected scholars. And quite suddenly the entire foundation of our national dialogue seems to have undergone a radical shift. The old fears that once preoccupied us—of nuclear annihilation or massive unemployment—have succumbed to a more insidious portent: We may be choking on our own concept of progress. Economic growth? What once seemed an unquestioned good is now being challenged as a positive evil. Live better electrically? We are now adjured to "save a watt." Bring your industry to our state (or county or city)? The signs now read: Keep Out.

A new set of priorities is taking shape before our eyes. The struggle to save the environment is no longer the par-

3

ticular concern of an embattled and little-heard fringe of society. As California's Democratic leader Jesse Unruh once put it, "Ecology has become the political substitute for the word *mother.*" But, however broadly concerned the people and the politicians, the extent of our troubles and the means of correcting them remain a subject of intense dispute among people of goodwill. Is man's survival literally at stake? If so, is zero population growth the answer, with all that it implies by way of a revolution in morals and mores? Where should we begin—by limiting our numbers or limiting that steady rise in the standard of living which most Americans now take for granted and for which impoverished people around the world—including those in our own country—still yearn? Having banned DDT, must we now ban the auto and its internal combustion engine as well? And beyond these considerations, can the technology that so many charge with destroying chances of survival actually be marshaled for our salvation?

Such issues are at the heart of the new dialogue and form the main concerns around which this compilation is built. The first section of this volume shocks us with some of the grimmest recent accounts of man's prospect for survival. The section is designed to spell out, in full and pessimistic detail, the fears and warnings that appear to preoccupy a growing segment of our intellectual and scientific community. The second section—which comes as something of an antidote—rings in the counterarguments to these visions of doom and, in a more hopeful vein, establishes the broad limits and basic framework within which the rest of the discussion progresses.

Accordingly, the third section focuses on what seems to be emerging as the central point around which the ecological debate can be expected to revolve in the years immediately ahead: the alleged virtues—and newly proclaimed vices—of economic growth, rising industrial production, and advancing technology. No country has yet put a ban on engineering studies within its borders, but such a possibility appears less fanciful with each passing day. In the fourth section some experts in the field present their views on the costs of putting things right and the priorities required to do it. The final section of this compilation strikes the more positive note sounded at the United Nations Conference on the Human Environment in Stockholm in the late spring of 1972. Everywhere, governments and individuals are moving to meet the challenge to survival with bold programs and a cooperative spirit. If the spirit of Stockholm endures, one may take heart in the belief that humanity may indeed prevail.

The compiler wishes to thank the authors and publishers who have courteously granted permission for the reprinting of their materials in this book. He is especially indebted to his wife, Stephanie, and to his son, Michael, for their cheerful assistance in the preparation of the manuscript.

WILLIAM P. LINEBERRY

November 1972

A NOTE TO THE READER

The reader's attention is directed to the following earlier Reference Shelf compilations which deal with aspects of the pollution problem: *The Water Crisis* (Volume 38, Number 6), edited by George A. Nikolaieff and published in 1967; *Protecting Our Environment* (Volume 42, Number 1), edited by Grant S. McClellan and published in 1970; and *Land Use in the United States* (Volume 43, Number 2), edited by Grant S. McClellan and published in 1971.

CONTENTS

IV. OF COSTS AND PRIORITIES

V. THE WAY AHEAD: SOME PROFFERED SOLUTIONS

I. CHALLENGE TO MAN'S SURVIVAL

EDITOR'S INTRODUCTION

The late Adlai Stevenson put it well: "We travel together, passengers on a little spaceship, dependent on its vulnerable supplies of air and soil . . . , preserved from annihilation only by the care, the work, and I say the love, we give our fragile craft." From the viewpoint of many critics of our current way of life, we are all of us guilty of grossly abusing our little spaceship, gouging our feckless graffiti upon its shell and generally deranging the delicate mechanism that makes it go. But ours is more than an aesthetic crime. The ancient maxim of the economist still applies: resources are scarce and limited absolutely; once they are used up, they are gone forever. Man cannot go on consuming voraciously, expanding constantly in numbers, and expect his world to provide ceaselessly and unerringly for his insatiable wants.

As the articles in this section point out, both science and logic attest to the fact that resources are fixed and absolute. We need only project slightly the ever mounting nature of our consumption of these resources to realize that exhaustion —and collapse—await us if we go on as we have been. What may be surprising is how near the day of judgment actually is, by some authorities' reckoning.

Here, then, is a predicament which knows no national boundaries or ideological affinities. Like some ominous freight train, disaster heads inexorably toward us even as we move along the tracks toward it. Practically speaking, there is no escaping except by switching tracks, a course two of the authors in this section strongly recommend. But there is a moral dimension to our predicament, as well. If the rest of the world consumed resources at the high rate the United States is consuming them, our day of judgment would vir-

tually be at hand. In other words, Americans enjoy their
rising standard of living only at the sufferance of a largely
impoverished and technologically undeveloped world. Who
is to right the imbalance before we are all carried to doom
—the poor and impoverished, who have so little effect on
our plight; or, the rich and affluent, who have so much?

The first article in this section caused something of a
sensation on both sides of the Atlantic when it first appeared
in Britain in early 1972. It stated the nature of the ecological
crisis in the most urgent and forceful terms seen to that date,
while setting forth a convincing, if harsh, blueprint for survival if historic necessity was to be cheated. The "Blueprint,"
as it has come to be known, marshals known facts in a particularly hair-raising fashion. The second article is hardly
less unnerving. It is the thesis of S. R. Eyre that man is a
species which is entering upon a "swarming stage" and that
unlike other species, whose swarming is limited by nature
in time and space, man can end by inundating both himself
and the world. A pessimist of the Malthusian school, Eyre
clearly views man's prospects for survival as exceedingly dim.

The last two articles in this section—from *The Economist* and *The Christian Science Monitor*—demonstrate that
the ecological crisis is worldwide in scope, being limited
neither to rich countries nor to poor, neither to Communist
regimes nor to a variety of liberal Western systems.

MUDDLING OUR WAY TO EXTINCTION [1]

The Need for Change

The principal defect of the industrial way of life with
its ethos of expansion is that it is not sustainable. Its termina-
tion within the lifetime of someone born today is inevitable
—unless it continues to be sustained for a while longer by an
entrenched minority at the cost of imposing great suffering
on the rest of mankind. We can be certain, however, that

[1] From *A Blueprint for Survival*, by the editors of *The Ecologist*.
Houghton. '72. Reprinted by permission of the publisher Houghton Mifflin
Company. Copyright © 1972.

sooner or later it will end (only the precise time and circumstances are in doubt), and that it will do so in one of two
ways: either against our will, in a succession of famines, epidemics, social crises and wars; or because we want it to—
because we wish to create a society which will not impose
hardship and cruelty upon our children—in a succession of
thoughtful, humane and measured changes. We believe that
a growing number of people are aware of this choice, and
are more interested in our proposals for creating a sustainable society than in yet another recitation of the reasons why
this should be done. . . .

Radical change is both necessary and inevitable because
the present increases in human numbers and per capita consumption, by disrupting ecosystems and depleting resources,
are undermining the very foundations of survival. At present
the world population of . . . [3.6 billion] is increasing by
2 percent per year (72 million), but this overall figure con-
ceals crucially important differences between countries. The
industrialized countries with one third of the world population have annual growth rates of between 0.5 and 1.0 percent; the undeveloped countries on the other hand, with
two thirds of the world population, have annual growth rates
of between 2 and 3 percent, and from 40 to 45 percent of
their populations is under fifteen. It is commonly overlooked
that in countries with an unbalanced age structure of this
kind the population will continue to increase for many years
even after fertility has fallen to the replacement level. As the
Population Council has pointed out: "If replacement is
achieved in the developed world by 2000 and in the developing world by 2040, then the world's population will stabilize
at nearly 15.5 billion . . . about a century hence, or well over
four times the present size."

The per capita use of energy and raw materials also shows
a sharp division between the developed and the undeveloped
parts of the world. Both are increasing their use of these
commodities, but consumption in the developed countries is
so much higher that, even with their smaller share of the

population, their consumption may well represent over 80 percent of the world total. For the same reason, similar percentage increases are far more significant in the developed countries; to take one example, between 1957 and 1967 per capita steel consumption rose by 12 percent in the United States and by 41 percent in India, but the actual increases (in kilograms per year) were from 568 to 634 and from 9.2 to 13 respectively. Nor is there any sign that an eventual end to economic growth is envisaged, and indeed industrial economies appear to break down if growth ceases or even slows, however high the absolute level of consumption. Even the United States still aims at an annual growth of GNP of 4 percent or more. Within this overall figure much higher growth rates occur for the use of particular resources, such as oil.

The Need for Change

The combination of human numbers and per capita consumption has a considerable impact on the environment, in terms of both the resources we take from it and the pollutants we impose on it. A distinguished group of scientists, who came together for a Study of Critical Environmental Problems (SCEP) under the auspices of the Massachusetts Institute of Technology, state in their report the clear need for a means of measuring this impact, and have coined the term *ecological demand,* which they define as "a summation of all man's demands on the environment, such as the extraction of resources and the return of wastes." [See "The Limits to Growth" in Section III, below, for a further discussion of this study.] Gross Domestic Product (GDP), which is population multiplied by material standard of living, appears to provide the most convenient measure of ecological demand, and according to the UN *Statistical Yearbook* this is increasing annually by 5 to 6 percent, or doubling every 13.5 years. If this trend should continue, then in the time taken for world population to double (which is estimated to be by just after the year 2000), total ecological demand will have increased by a factor of six. SCEP estimates that "such demand-producing activities as agriculture, mining and industry have global annual rates of increase of 3.5 percent and 7 percent respectively. An integrated rate of increase is estimated to be between 5 and 6 percent per year, in comparison with an annual rate of population increase of only 2 percent."

It should go without saying that the world cannot accommodate this continued increase in ecological demand. *Indefinite* growth of whatever type cannot be sustained by *finite* resources. This is the nub of the environmental predicament. It is still less possible to maintain indefinite *exponential* growth—and unfortunately the growth of ecological demand is proceeding exponentially (i.e. it is increasing geometrically, by compound interest).

The implications of exponential growth are not generally appreciated and are well worth considering. As Professor [Jay] Forrester [of the Massachusetts Institute of Technology] explains it,

Pure exponential growth possesses the characteristic of behaving according to a "doubling time." Each fixed time interval shows a doubling of the relevant system variable. Exponential growth is treacherous and misleading. A system variable can continue through many doubling intervals without seeming to reach significant size. But then in one or two more doubling periods, still following the same law of exponential growth, it suddenly seems to become overwhelming.

Thus, supposing world petroleum reserves stood at 2,100 billion barrels, and supposing our rate of consumption was increasing by 6.9 percent per year, then . . . demand will exceed supply by the end of the century. What is significant, however, is not the speed at which such vast reserves can be depleted, but that as late as 1975 there will appear to be reserves fully ample enough to last for considerably longer. Such a situation can easily lull one into a false sense of security and the belief that a given growth rate can be sustained, if not indefinitely, at least for a good deal longer than is actually the case. The same basic logic applies to the availability of any resource including land, and it is largely because of this particular dynamic of exponential growth that the environmental predicament has come upon us so suddenly, and why its solution requires urgent and radical measures, many of which run counter to values which, in our industrial society we have been taught to regard as fundamental.

If we allow the present growth rate to persist, total ecological demand will increase by a factor of thirty-two over the next sixty-six years—and there can be no serious person today willing to concede the possibility, or indeed the desirability, of our accommodating the pressures arising from such growth. For this can be done only at the cost of disrupting ecosystems and exhausting resources, which must lead to the failure of food supplies and the collapse of society. It is worth briefly considering each in turn.

Disruption of Ecosystems

We depend for our survival on the predictability of ecological processes. If they were at all arbitrary, we would not know when to reap or sow, and we would be at the mercy of environmental whim. We could learn nothing about the rest of nature, advance no hypotheses, suggest no "laws." Fortunately, ecological processes *are* predictable, and although theirs is a relatively young discipline, ecologists have been able to formulate a number of important "laws," one of which in particular relates to environmental predictability: namely, that all ecosystems tend towards stability, and further that the more diverse and complex the ecosystem the more stable it is; that is, the more species there are, and the more they interrelate, the more stable is their environment. By stability is meant the ability to return to the original position after any change, instead of being forced into a totally different pattern—and hence predictability.

Unfortunately, we behave as if we knew nothing of the environment and had no conception of its predictability, treating it instead with scant and brutal regard as if it were an idiosyncratic and extremely stupid slave. We seem never to have reflected on the fact that a tropical rain forest supports innumerable insect species and yet is never devastated by them; that its rampant luxuriance is not contingent on our overflying it once a month and bombarding it with insecticides, herbicides, fungicides, and what-have-you. And yet we tremble over our wheatfields and cabbage patches with a desperate battery of synthetic chemicals, in an absurd attempt to impede the operation of the immutable "law" we have just mentioned—that all ecosystems tend towards stability, therefore diversity and complexity, therefore a growing number of different plant and animal species until a climax or optimal condition is achieved. If we were clever, we would recognize that successful long-term agriculture demands the achievement of an artificial climax, an imitation of the pre-existing ecosystem, so that the level of unwanted species could be controlled by those that did no harm to the crop plants.

Instead we have put our money on pesticides, which although they have been effective, have been so only to a limited and now diminishing extent: according to SCEP, the 34 percent increase in world food production from 1951 to 1966 required increased investments in nitrogenous fertilizers of 146 percent and in pesticides of 300 percent. At the same time they have created a number of serious problems, notably resistance—some 250 pest species are resistant to one group of pesticides or another, while many others require increased applications to keep their populations within manageable proportions—and the promotion of formerly innocuous species to pest proportions, because the predators that formerly kept them down have been destroyed. The spread of DDT and other organochlorines in the environment has resulted in alarming population declines among woodcock, grebes, various birds of prey and seabirds, and in a number of fish species, principally the sea trout. SCEP comments:

The oceans are an ultimate accumulation site of DDT and its residues. As much as 25 percent of the DDT compounds produced to date may have been transferred to the sea. The amount in the marine biota is estimated to be in the order of less than 0.1 percent of total production and has already produced a demonstrable impact upon the marine environment. . . . The decline in productivity of marine food fish and the accumulation of levels of DDT in their tissues which are unacceptable to man can only be accelerated by DDT's continued release to the environment. . . ."

There are half a million man-made chemicals in use today, yet we cannot predict the behavior or properties of the greater part of them (either singly or in combination) once they are released into the environment. We know, however, that the combined effects of pollution and habitat destruction menace the survival of no less than 280 mammal, 350 bird, and 20,000 plant species. To those who regret these losses but greet them with the comment that the survival of *Homo sapiens* is surely more important than that of an eagle or a primrose, we repeat that *Homo sapiens* himself depends on the continued resilience of those ecological networks of which eagles and primroses are integral parts. We do not need to utterly destroy the ecosphere to bring catastrophe upon ourselves: all we have to do is to carry on as we are, clearing forests, "reclaiming" wetlands, and imposing sufficient quantities of pesticides, radioactive materials, plastics, sewage, and industrial wastes upon our air, water and land systems to make them inhospitable to the species on which their continued stability and integrity depend. Industrial man in the world today is like a bull in a china shop, with the single difference that a bull with half the information about the properties of china as we have about those of ecosystems would probably try and adapt its behavior to its environment rather than the reverse. By contrast, *Homo sapiens industrialis* is determined that the china shop should adapt to him, and has therefore set himself the goal of reducing it to rubble in the shortest possible time.

Failure of Food Supplies

Increases in food production in the undeveloped world have barely kept abreast of population growth. Such increases as there have been are due not to higher productivity but to the opening up of new land for cultivation. Unfortunately this will not be possible for much longer: all the good land in the world is now being farmed, and according to the FAO [Food and Agriculture Organization of the United Nations], at present rates of expansion none of the marginal land that is left will be unfarmed by 1985—indeed some of the land now under cultivation has been so exhausted that it will have to be returned to permanent pasture.

For this reason, FAO's program to feed the world depends on a program of intensification, at the heart of which are the new high-yield varieties of wheat and rice. These are highly responsive to inorganic fertilizers and quick-maturing, so that up to ten times present yields can be obtained from them. Unfortunately, they are highly vulnerable to disease, and therefore require increased protection by pesticides, and of course they demand massive inputs of fertilizers (up to twenty-seven times present ones). Not only will these disrupt local ecosystems, thereby jeopardizing long-term productivity, but they force hard-pressed undeveloped nations to rely on the agrochemical industries of the developed world.

Whatever their virtues and faults, the new genetic hybrids are not intended to solve the world food problem, but only to give us time to devise more permanent and realistic solutions. It is our view, however, that these hybrids are not the best means of doing this, since their use is likely to bring about a reduction in overall diversity, when the clear need is to develop an agriculture diverse enough to have long-term potential. We must beware of those "experts" who appear to advocate the transformation of the ecosphere into nothing more than a food-factory for man. The concept of a world consisting solely of man and a few favored food plants is so ludicrously impracticable as to be seriously contemplated only by those who find solace in their own willful ignorance of the real world of biological diversity.

We in Britain must bear in mind that we depend on imports for half our food, and that we are unlikely to improve on this situation. The 150,000 acres which are lost from agriculture each year are about 70 percent more productive than the average for all enclosed land, while we are already beginning to experience diminishing returns from the use of inorganic fertilizers. In the period 1964-1969, applications of phosphates have gone up by 2 percent, potash by 7 percent, and nitrogen by 40 percent, yet yields per acre of wheat, barley, lucerne [alfalfa] and temporary grass have leveled off and are beginning to decline, while that of permanent grass has risen only slightly and may be leveling off. As per capita food availability declines throughout the rest of the world, and it appears inevitable it will, we will find it progressively more difficult and expensive to meet our food requirements from abroad. The prospect of severe food shortages within the next thirty years is not so much a fantasy as that of the continued abundance promised us by so many of our politicians.

Exhaustion of Resources

As we have seen, continued exponential growth of consumption of materials and energy is impossible. Present reserves of all but a few metals will be exhausted within fifty years, if consumption rates continue to grow as they are. Obviously there will be new discoveries and advances in mining technology, but these are likely to provide us with only a limited stay of execution. Synthetics and substitutes are likely to be of little help, since they must be made from materials which themselves are in short supply; while the hoped-for availability of unlimited energy would not be the answer, since the problem is the ratio of useful metal to waste matter (which would have to be disposed of without disrupting ecosystems), not the need for cheap power. Indeed, the availability of unlimited power holds more of a threat than a promise, since energy use is inevitably polluting, and in addition we would ultimately have to face the problem of disposing of an intractable amount of waste heat.

The developed nations consume such disproportionate amounts of protein, raw materials and fuels that unless they considerably reduce their consumption there is no hope of the undeveloped nations markedly improving their standards of living. This vast differential is a cause of much and growing discontent, made worse by our attempts at cultural uniformity on behalf of an expanding market economy. In the end, we are altering people's aspirations without providing the means for them to be satisfied. In the rush to industrialize we break up communities, so that the controls which formerly regulated behavior are destroyed before alternatives can be provided. Urban drift is one result of this process, with a consequent rise in antisocial practices, crime, delinquency, and so on, which are so costly for society in terms both of money and of well-being.

At the same time, we are sowing the seeds of massive unemployment by increasing the ratio of capital to labor so that the provision of each job becomes ever more expensive. In a world of fast diminishing resources, we shall quickly come to the point when very great numbers of people will be thrown out of work, when the material compensations of urban life are either no longer available or prohibitively expensive, and consequently when whole sections of society will find good cause to express their considerable discontent in ways likely to be anything but pleasant for their fellows.

It is worth bearing in mind that the barriers between us and epidemics are not so strong as is commonly supposed. Not only is it increasingly difficult to control the vectors of disease, but it is more than probable that urban populations are being insidiously weakened by overall pollution levels, even when they are not high enough to be incriminated in any one illness. At the same time international mobility speeds the spread of disease. With this background, and at a time of widespread public demoralization, the collapse of vital social services such as power and sanitation, could easily provoke a series of epidemics—and we cannot say with confidence that we would be able to cope with them.

At times of great distress and social chaos, it is more than probable that governments will fall into the hands of reckless and unscrupulous elements, who will not hesitate to threaten neighboring governments with attack, if they feel that they can wrest from them a larger share of the world's vanishing resources. Since a growing number of countries (an estimated thirty-six by 1980) will have nuclear power stations, and therefore sources of plutonium for nuclear warheads, the likelihood of a whole series of local (if not global) nuclear engagements is greatly increased. . . .

Conclusion

. . . . There will be those who regard these accounts of the consequences of trying to accommodate present growth rates as fanciful. But the imaginative leap from the available scientific information to such predictions is negligible, compared with that required for those alternative predictions, laughably considered "optimistic," of a world of 10 to 15 billion people, all with the same material standard of living as the United States, on a concrete replica of this planet, the only moving parts being their machines and possibly themselves. Faced with inevitable change, we have to make decisions, and we must make these decisions *soberly* in the light of the best information, and not as if we were caricatures of the archetypal mad scientist.

By now it should be clear that the main problems of the environment do not arise from temporary and accidental malfunctions of existing economic and social systems. On the contrary, they are the warning signs of a profound incompatibility between deeply rooted beliefs in continuous growth and the dawning recognition of the earth as a spaceship, limited in its resources and vulnerable to thoughtless mishandling. The nature of our response to these symptoms is crucial. If we refuse to recognize the cause of our trouble, the result can only be increasing disillusion and growing strain upon the fragile institutions that maintain external peace and internal social cohesion. If, on the other hand, we can respond to this unprecedented challenge with informed and constructive action, the rewards will be as great as the penalties for failure. . . .

We believe that if a strategy for survival is to have any chance of success, the solutions must be formulated in the light of the problems and not from a timorous and superficial understanding of what may or may not be immediately feasible. If we plan remedial action with our eyes on political rather than ecological reality, then very reasonably, very practicably, and very surely, we will muddle our way to extinction.

A measure of political reality is that government has yet to acknowledge the impending crisis. This is to some extent because it has given itself no machinery for looking at energy, resources, food, environmental disruption and social disruption as a whole, as part of a general, global pattern, preferring instead to deal with its many aspects as if they were self-contained analytical units. Lord Rothschild's Central Policy Review Staff in the Cabinet Office, which is the only body in [Britain's] government which might remedy the situation, appears not to think it worthwhile: at the moment at least, they are undertaking "no specific studies on the environment that would require an environmentalist or ecologist." There is a strong element of positive feedback here, in that there can be no appreciation of our predicament unless we view it in totality, and yet government can see no cause to do so unless it can be shown that such a predicament exists.

Possibly because government sees the world in fragments and not as a totality, it is difficult to detect in its actions or words any coherent general policy, although both major political parties appear to be mesmerized by two dominating notions: that economic expansion is essential for survival and is the best possible index of progress and well-being; and that unless solutions can be devised that do not threaten this notion, then the problems should not be regarded as existing. Unfortunately, government has an increasingly powerful incentive for continued expansion in the tendency for economic growth to create the need for more economic growth. This it does in six ways:

Firstly, the introduction of technological devices, i.e. the growth of the technosphere, can only occur to the detriment of the ecosphere, which means that it leads to the destruction of natural controls which must then be replaced by further technological ones. It is in this way that pesticides and artificial fertilizers create the need for yet more pesticides and artificial fertilizers.

Secondly, for various reasons, industrial growth, particularly in its earlier phases, promotes population growth. Even in its later phases, this can still occur at a high rate (0.5 percent in the UK). Jobs must constantly be created for the additional people—not just any job, but those that are judged acceptable in terms of current values. This basically means that the capital outlay per person employed must be maintained, otherwise the level of "productivity" per man will fall, which is a determinant of both the "viability" of economic enterprise and of the "standard of living."

Thirdly, no government can hope to survive widespread and protracted unemployment, and without changing the basis of our industrial society, the only way government can prevent it is by stimulating economic growth.

Fourthly, business enterprises, whether state-owned or privately owned, tend to become self-perpetuating, which means that they require surpluses for further investment. This favors continued growth.

Fifthly, the success of a government and its ability to obtain support is to a large extent assessed in terms of its ability to increase the "standard of living" as measured by per capita gross national product (GNP).

Finally, confidence in the economy, which is basically a function of its ability to grow, must be maintained to ensure a healthy state of the stock market. Were confidence to fall, stock values would crash, drastically reducing the availability of capital for investment and hence further growth, which would lead to further unemployment. This would result in a further fall in stock-market values and hence give rise to a positive-feedback chain-reaction, which under the existing order might well lead to social collapse.

For all these reasons, we can expect our government (whether Conservative or Labour) to encourage further increases in GNP regardless of the consequences, which in any case tame "experts" can be found to play down. It will curb growth only when public opinion demands such a move, in which case it will be politically expedient, and when a method is found for doing so without creating unemployment or excessive pressure on capital. We believe this is possible only within the framework of a fully integrated plan.

The emphasis must be on integration. If we develop relatively clean technologies but do not end economic growths then sooner or later we will find ourselves with as great a pollution problem as before but without the means of tackling it. If we stabilize our economies and husband our nonrenewable resources without stabilizing our populations we will find we are no longer able to feed ourselves. . . .

Our task is to create a society which is sustainable and which will give the fullest possible satisfaction to its members. Such a society by definition would depend not on expansion but on stability. This does not mean to say that it would be stagnant—indeed it could well afford more variety than does the state of uniformity at present being imposed by the pursuit of technological efficiency. We believe that the stable society, . . . as well as removing the sword of Damocles which hangs over the heads of future generations, is much more likely than the present one to bring the peace and fulfillment which hitherto have been regarded, sadly as utopian.

MAN THE PEST [2]

The present state of the whole of the human species in relation to its total environment is so vast a topic that cautious and discriminating people might well avoid it as the subject of a single, short paper. It is, after all, a major area of concern for many sciences—social, biological, and technological. I take it as my subject here not, I hope, because I am incautious or undiscriminating, but because the ecology of any species, no matter how complex its behavior, can justifiably be regarded as unitary, and should therefore be reviewed as a whole from time to time. Furthermore, I would hold that the predicament of our species at the present time makes such a review not only desirable but vital.

Following an evolution of hundreds of millennia, *Homo sapiens* emerged on the postglacial scene as a dominant species with almost worldwide distribution. Clearly his numbers had increased only very slowly over this vast period of time, and it was not until around A.D. 1810 that a world population of one billion was first achieved. Only just over a century then elapsed before the species had added just as many again to its numbers, the two-billion mark being passed just after 1920. Then, in less than forty years, another increment of the same magnitude was added by the end of 1960.

If the growth rate of the decade 1950-60 were to be continued up to A.D. 2000, projection indicates the addition of further increments of one billion by the years 1975, 1984, 1992, and 1998, and a total of 7.41 billion by the end of the century. In fact it seems unlikely that such a growth rate could be sustained. Nevertheless, realistic projections made in 1963 still indicated a vast population increase by the year 2000; projections for that year varied between 5.3 billion and 6.83 billion according to the assumptions made, but medium assumptions indicated a population of 4 billion by about

[2] From "Man the Pest: The Dim Chance of Survival," by S. R. Eyre, senior lecturer in geography at the University of Leeds in England. *New York Review of Books*. 17:18-27. N. 18, '71. Reprinted with permission from *The New York Review of Books*. Copyright © 1971. The author is the coeditor of *Geography as Human Ecology*.

1977, 5 billion by about 1990, and 5.96 billion by the end of the century. Furthermore, there are now clear indications that, in the absence of disasters on a world scale, these 1963 medium estimates will be far exceeded and that the world population in A.D. 2000 will be more than double that in 1960.

The Swarming Stage

A biologist presented with this graph of population increase would diagnose a "swarming stage" situation. This is frequently observed both in nature and in the laboratory when a population of a particular species experiences favorable environmental conditions in the absence of some of the environmental controls to which it has normally been subjected throughout its evolution. The stage is inevitably short-lived and may be terminated in a number of ways: there may be mass neurosis owing to overcrowding, as has been suggested for the Scandinavian lemming; there may be a great increase in predators; or there may occur that concatenation of events which is so well demonstrated in a laboratory culture of bacteria, where the population gradually expands to occupy the whole medium and then rapidly declines from the original focus outward, partly through food shortage and partly poisoned by its own waste products. Whatever the end may be, the inevitable outcome is mass mortality.

Social scientists have largely been very unwilling to view the increase of our own species on so cataclysmic a plane. They have held that man has evaded the inexorable operation of the Malthusian law (and other biological controls) by his creation of a technology which can be handed on from generation to generation with increasing refinement and elaboration. In the minds of many people, however, doubts are beginning to develop. Even for one who has almost boundless faith in technological advancement, though it may be possible to contemplate with equanimity a world population of over 6 billion in A.D. 2000, it becomes progressively more difficult to be optimistic about 12 billion in

2035, 25 billion by 2065, and 50 billion by around the end of the twenty-first century.

Fallacies About Economic Growth

Because rational projections can produce figures such as these, for a point in time only four generations ahead, an increasing number of social scientists are concluding that some kind of population limitation program will have to be formulated. Unfortunately, those who have begun to recognize the need for such a limitation often seem to betray a lack of appreciation of the complexity of the whole problem: indeed their recommendations are often misleading if not actually contradictory. Thus we read:

> Increasing rates of economic growth and slowing rates of population growth are both essential to rising levels of living.—Irene B. Taeuber. *Future Population Trends and Prospects*

Statements such as this must be regarded as misleading since they may leave the reader with the impression that, unlike population growth, economic growth may well be infinite. And yet the very reason why population increase must cease is *because* economic growth is *finite*. Although growth has become the cornerstone of our technological society, nevertheless any vision of its continuance into the indefinite future is based on illusion. All the evidence suggests that the earth's resources, renewable and nonrenewable, cannot possibly sustain technological and agricultural expansion for very much longer.

Agricultural Food Production

In order to justify this statement fully, it would be necessary to review the whole of the earth's resources alongside the population projections already given. Clearly this is impossible in the space available, but examination of a selection of critical facts and basic issues provides sufficient indication of the gravity of the human situation. The rapid rate of population increase in many of the technology-deficient nations is one of the most striking features of the world population picture. It is particularly obvious in the countries of southern and eastern Asia where, on the basis of the medium projection, a 1970 population of some 2 billion will increase to some 3.4 billion by A.D. 2000.

We are concerned here then with more than half of the world's population. Work that has been done on the rates of increase in food production in this area provides no grounds whatever for optimism. One set of projections for India indicated that while the population would have increased 2.9 times by the end of the fifty-year period following 1961, the available food supply would be capable of increasing only 2.74 times. Furthermore this estimate was assuming the realization of the "full potential of increased agricultural production" making the best possible use of known technology and allowing for little administrative or cultural waste. It should also be noted that, even if this level of productivity were achieved, production would still fall short of a satisfactory nutrition level by something like 20 percent. In fact, during the five years following the publication of these projections, agricultural production in India fell far short of the rate prescribed for it: there is no indication whatever that the near-miracle of technological application and administrative efficiency can possibly be achieved.

Working on similar assumptions, . . . [P. V. Sukhatme and W. Schulte] estimated that the Far East would require an increase in food supplies of 286 percent between 1960 and 2000 in order to achieve an adequate nutritional standard, and that the developing countries as a whole would require an increase of 261 percent. He went on to make the point that, with considerable effort, food production in the developing countries might be increased by 70 percent by 1980, but that food demands (taking into account population increase and a modest improvement in diet) will have risen by 100 percent. He emphasized, of course, that these broad figures conceal a variety of conditions, and that it is in Asia that the great difficulties will develop.

It seems most unlikely therefore that food production in Asia, even on the basis of the most optimistic assumptions regarding technological application and social adjustment, will be able to keep pace with population increase; and with any kind of climatic, economic, or social cataclysm, the shortfall will be enormous. Indeed it appears only reasonable to anticipate the necessity to obtain sufficient food for something like 700 million people in monsoon Asia by A.D. 2000, and if technical improvement and innovation proceed no faster than they have been doing during the past twenty-five years, much greater deficits will have developed.

Food imports on a vast scale would be necessary to counterbalance deficits of this size. Whether or not these could materialize would depend upon two things: first, the existence of commensurate food surpluses elsewhere in the world, and secondly the long-term ability of the Asian peoples to purchase them. With regard to the first point, any attempt to provide a simple answer would be hazardous; nevertheless, some commonly held views on the agricultural potential of the earth require closer scrutiny.

It is certainly true that the best lands of Europe and eastern North America are, at the present time, capable of producing large agricultural surpluses—indeed overproduction has been a frequent problem. In the work already cited, Sukhatme estimates that by 1980 this surplus could amount to about 10 percent of world food production and that this would approximately balance the food deficit in Asia and elsewhere. Whether the volume of this food transfer could go on progressively up to the year 2000 is very problematical: the projected population increase in the developed countries would certainly take care of a lot of surpluses, and the attitudes of the taxpayers in the producing countries would become a not inconsiderable factor should the transfer be effected as aid rather than through trade.

The Potential Productivity of Virgin Lands

It is also important to examine some of the fairly deep-rooted misconceptions regarding the large, sparsely populated areas of the earth. Quite a large percentage of these are arid deserts, mountain ranges, and cold tundras which could only be made productive with a capital input which would be prohibitive even for a rich, technologically developed nation. At first glance, however, suggestions regarding the potential productivity of the Amazon and Congo basins, Borneo, and the coastlands of New Guinea are more beguiling: these, after all, are well-watered tropical areas with high temperatures throughout the year. . . . If large-scale food production . . . were attempted [in such areas] without the necessary capital input, the resulting erosion . . . and general degradation would create more of a Pandora's Box than an Open Sesame.

The basic unrealism of any agricultural philosophy that visualizes a great increase in the use of mineral fertilizers by the underdeveloped countries is underlined by the pattern of phosphate consumption at the present time. Of all the mineral fertilizers, phosphates are the most important: they not only contain one of the vital elements for plant nutrition but also are essential for the rapid incorporation of atmospheric nitrogen into the nutrient cycle through the medium of leguminous plants. And yet mineral phosphates in economically exploitable deposits are of very restricted distribution: over the past decade 90 percent of world production has come from the United States, the USSR, Morocco, and Tunisia, and world reserves are of very limited extent.

Furthermore, in the year 1968-69, out of a world consumption of 17.3 million metric tons (P_2O_5 from all sources), Anglo-America, the USSR, and Europe accounted for 13.1 mmt and the agriculture of the whole of Africa, Latin America, and Asia (less Japan and mainland China) less than 2.2 mmt. The agriculture of West Germany (population 60 million) consumed twice as much as the combined agricultural systems of India, Pakistan, and Indonesia (population over 700 million). One must doubt the feasibility of so expensive a commodity being made available in vast quantities to poor countries.

Food from the Oceans

The oceans have often been presented as a limitless source of food with which to supplement terrestrial production, but recent estimates have shown this to be very unrealistic. Precision is impossible at the present time, but the fact that estimates based on two independent approaches have produced very similar answers does indicate that we now have a sound notion of the total productivity of the earth's water bodies.

A summation of the productivity of the upper trophic levels of marine life has produced answers of between 300 and 320 mmt per annum, of which no more than half—150-160 mmt—are harvestable at a sustained yield. When we recollect that the total world catch of aquatic products in 1966 was already in the vicinity of 60 mmt, it becomes patently obvious that here is no limitless supply. It would certainly be possible to push production up to 100 mmt by A.D. 2000 if the capital were made available, but this would only be a 66 ⅔ percent increase on the present and there is reason to believe it could only be achieved by a total physical investment in ships and equipment of three times that of the present (an increase of 200 percent). If an attempt were then made to push production to its probable limit of about 150 mmt this might well require six times the present investment.

This is obviously not an inexpensive way by which impoverished nations can supplement their food supplies. It is equally clear that any attempt to increase marine production by mass harvesting of the lower trophic levels of the food pyramid, such as the plankton and small plankton feeders, would be even more costly per unit of production, quite apart from the fact that conventional fishing would then become less profitable as the basis of fish subsistence was removed.

It has also been suggested that the productivity of the oceans could be increased by raising the nutrient status of the water. This is undeniably feasible but its implementation begs so many of the questions that have already been raised that it cannot seriously be entertained as a substantial contribution to world food problems over the next twenty-five to fifty years. Indeed, there is every indication that population increase and human technology on the land masses are far more likely to *decrease* the productivity of the water bodies than the reverse. Methyl mercury in the oceans, the eutrophication of Lake Erie, and the deleterious effects of chlorinated hydrocarbons on marine plankton—these are all now well-worn themes.

Furthermore, concentrated pollution of the more insidious kind is being discharged into the marine ecosystems, at the present time, by a relatively small percentage of the world's rivers—primarily those of North America and Europe. If, in an effort to raise agricultural productivity, the other peoples of the world begin to apply biocides to the land in anything like the same concentration, the effect could be very serious. If these peoples also expand their industrial capacity and begin to emit industrial waste in materially greater quantities, then the results could be catastrophic.

World Consumption of Minerals

For reasons I am about to give, there may well be no chance of such worldwide industrialization. From the viewpoint of the ultimate ecological health of the world this could be one of the most fortunate facets of the human situation, but one cannot expect the technology-deficient nations to take this view: at the present time it is the lack of a capacity to produce industrial goods that is regarded as the main criterion of "underdevelopment," and those impoverished nations with large food deficits will obviously attempt to expand industrial production as one means of increasing their economic flexibility and exchange capability.

At the present time, although a large percentage of the world's industrial raw materials are extracted in underdeveloped countries, these materials are largely consumed by the manufacturing industries of Europe and North America. This applies not only to obvious commodities such as iron ore but to almost the whole range of mineral materials which are indispensable to the functioning of a modern industrial complex. Detailed and accurate statistics for the *consumption* of such commodities are notoriously difficult to obtain, but a few examples make the broad picture clear enough.

In 1965, out of a world smelter production of about six million tons of metallic copper, the industries of Europe, the USSR, and the United States (total population about 850 million) consumed well over 75 percent while the industries of the whole of Asia, Africa, and Latin America (population about 2.5 billion) consumed far less than 25 percent. Indeed if the very considerable copper consumption of Japan and the Union of South Africa is deducted, an almost insignificant amount is left to the underdeveloped world.

More precise figures are available for the world consumption of tin. In 1967 the industries of the non-Communist world (along with Yugoslavia) consumed 166,000 short tons of which almost 75 percent was absorbed by Western Europe and Anglo-America alone and less than 10 percent by Southern Asia, Africa, and Latin America. And in the case of aluminum the contrast between the developed and the underdeveloped world is even more striking: out of a world production of 7.415 million short tons in 1965, Europe, Anglo-America, and the USSR consumed about 7 million tons and Japan a further 300,000 tons. Even in the absence of exact consumption figures for the technology-deficient countries it is obvious that their industries can have consumed only a negligible amount.

Some measure of the contrast between the technologically developed and the technology-deficient countries is obtained from the fact that the industries of the United States consume 50 percent of the annual world production of aluminum, 25 percent of the smelted copper, about 40 percent of the lead, over 36 percent of the nickel and zinc, and about 30 percent of the chromium. But it is perhaps even more salutary to realize that the industries of the Netherlands (population 13 million) consumed more tin than the whole of the Indian subcontinent (population 600 million) in 1967, and nearly twice as much as the whole of Africa (population 280 million).

It is against this background that we should view the future of living standards in underdeveloped countries. Many social scientists seem to regard it as axiomatic that these countries should industrialize at the maximum possible rate, presumably with a view to achieving Western levels ultimately. Before one commits oneself to this view, however, consideration should be given to the *amounts* of raw materials that would be required to achieve the Western scale of industrialization in technology-deficient areas.

During the century from 1860 to 1960, in which its population grew from about 31 million to 180 million, the United States consumed an estimated 45 million short tons of primary copper. If the population of the Indian subcontinent, *given no increase whatever,* were to use primary copper at the same rate per capita as did that of the United States in the 1960s, during the coming century it would consume 450 million tons. If the remainder of the technology-deficient countries were to do the same thing, they would consume about 1.25 billion tons. Inevitably the question arises whether there is so much copper available in the earth's crust; are there the amounts of lead, tin, zinc, cobalt, manganese, and tungsten for their rates of extraction to be raised commensurately? And if there are enough metals, are there sufficient power supplies to drive the machines that would be manufactured?

Unfortunately there are, as yet, no precise answers to these questions, but increasingly intensive and comprehensive exploration is beginning to provide some indication of the size of many mineral reserves. The problem is not merely one of geological exploration however: nearly all elements are *present* in nearly all rocks, but usually in such small proportions as to make them economically unexploitable. In the case of many metals, relatively rich ores are of very limited extent and will soon be worked out; from then onward cost will make them unavailable to all but the richest nations.

Since 1940 technology has consumed more primary metal than during the whole of previous history. During the past ten years world production of industrial metals has been increasing at a rate of more than 6 percent per annum. The situation is already an urgent one with regard to certain scarce metals which, though only used in small quantities, are nevertheless vital to industrial complexes. The world production of mercury in 1969 stood at about 275,000 flasks (76 lbs.) per annum, and the United States Bureau of Mines estimated world reserves, at $200 per flask, to be no more than 3.16 million flasks. At this price and with world demand rising at no more than half its present rate, far more mercury would have to be mined over the next twenty years than is present on the basis of this estimate. If world prices were to rise to over $1,000 per flask, leaner ores could be exploited and world production might be maintained for fifty years; but the future of industrial development in technology-deficient countries is obviously in great jeopardy if prices rise in this way.

To a greater or lesser degree one can speak of the imminent exhaustion of the reserves of a large number of essential metals; the time scale with which the crisis is concerned is to be measured in decades rather than centuries. One can appreciate why so eminent a figure as the former Director of the United States Bureau of Mines, Walter Hibbard, should have reached the conclusion that the time is rapidly approaching when indifference could be disastrous.

The all too prevalent notion that mineral resources are to all intents and purposes inexhaustible must be discarded with the least possible delay.

Energy Problems

A recent review of the world's energy resources reinforces Hibbard's statement. Technology today is very dependent on fossil fuels, particularly coal and oil. Although, given time, these could be substantially supplemented and partially replaced by other sources of energy, contemporary solar energy, direct and indirect, cannot be harnessed to the extent that it could supply total requirements, even with the present world population. The vista of a great world industrial complex supplied by tidal power and vast batteries of photoelectric cells is an illusion, and potentialities for hydroelectric generation, though much greater, are nevertheless subject to certain limitations: although total world *potential* is certainly equal to the present world consumption of energy, it is very unequally distributed, and the great majority of impounded reservoirs do, after all, become silted up during the course of a century or two.

Nor can nuclear sources be regarded as a certain future source of almost unlimited, cheap energy as has so frequently been assumed. Apart from problems of waste disposal, it is by no means certain that power from fusion reaction will ever be available and, indeed, the whole future of fission energy is now in dire jeopardy: consumption of the relatively rare uranium-235 in nonbreeder reactors could result in its complete exhaustion in relatively cheap deposits in a mere fraction of a century, resulting in a situation where nuclear power would be *more* expensive than power from fossil fuels and water.

One point is salient in this general picture: world reserves of petroleum—the mineral upon which world industry (particularly its transport sector) leans so heavily—are running out very rapidly. Evaluations from a range of estimates indicate quite clearly that the oil reserves of the United States (excluding Alaska) had been reduced by half by about the year 1968, and that only 10 percent will remain by about the year 1990. Equivalent estimates of world resources show that they will have been halved by a point in time somewhere between 1988 and A.D. 2000 with 90 percent exhaustion somewhere between the years 2020 and 2030. The main corollary is that world oil production will begin to fall at the turn of the century if not well before it.

The prospect of an almost doubled world population along with a decreasing supply of petroleum in a mere thirty years' time should be a daunting one for any technologist; indeed the shortness of the time interval is the most disconcerting point of all. When one considers the small amount of fundamental change in the resource basis of industry that has occurred in the past quarter of a century and compares it with the enormous revolution that appears to be necessary over the next quarter, the tasks ahead seem insuperable.

The case of the hydrocarbon fuels illustrates the point very well. It is true that the earth's reserves of tar sands and bituminous coal are sufficient to supply requirements for several centuries, given the present rate of expansion. But the costs of transport and plant conversion that would be necessary to distill a large percentage of the earth's supply of liquid fuels from such materials would be enormous. Furthermore, such rapid developments can usually only be achieved with the accumulated capital and technical skills of an already developed country; again, the technology-deficient countries will be at a great disadvantage, and one can visualize this being particularly serious if it coincided with a great increase in the cost of nuclear energy.

Optimism

With a hazard of these dimensions looming ahead one might expect that our species, unique in the animal kingdom for its capability for logical anticipation, would already be caught up in a near-frenzy of conservationist activity. In reality it is difficult to find serious public warnings, much less any sign of action. It is as though mankind has developed a blind faith in the immortality of the Industrial Revolution: ever since the great expansion began over a century and a half ago materials have been available, and it is unthinkable that this should not always be the case! Technology is taken to be omniscient, and even if resources are used up, substitutes will inevitably be found!

It is this faith in unspecified future technological innovation that is perhaps the most disturbing feature of our current social philosophy. It is completely unscientific and should certainly be deprecated by a body such as the British Association for the Advancement of Science. Any planning policy whose main prop rests upon unknowns rather than on rational assessment of what is known and understood indulges in nothing better than foolish optimism; its standpoint is exactly analogous to that of Mr. Micawber, but the evidence suggests that it has far less chance than he that something will actually turn up.

Pessimism

Before us there is a vision of what intellectual and material emancipation we, mankind, might achieve, and there is no technological reason why this should not materialize were *we* not so numerous. Indeed, just what might become possible, given time, cannot be imagined: a minority of mankind has already profited enormously after a mere century of development. But the press of numbers gives us so little time, and the door will inevitably close on the vast range of options open to mankind unless a revolution of unprecedented speed in attitudes and activities takes place within the next generation.

If the door does close, it will do so on an organism that is then forced into the position of having to destroy the remaining fertility of the planet in a vain effort to survive. The last precious resources will be used up carelessly and the very material that should be carefully husbanded will continue to contaminate the environment and vitiate the situation. As with the bacterial culture already referred to, an ultimate population crash to very low levels will be inevitable. Even if our species survives, the struggle back to a technological civilization will be subject to far greater restrictions than was originally the case. Nearly all easily accessible minerals will have been exhausted and the gene pool of the earth's ecosystems will be enormously reduced as compared to that which was available to man when he set out on his hunting and collecting forays in Paleolithic times.

This is no fanciful excursion into science fiction: given a continuation of present trends it is probably the most optimistic way of speaking of man's future. When the swarming stage is reached in nature, mass mortality is inevitable. But in nature, because of limited mobility, predators, and weather fluctuations, the effect of the swarm is rarely more than very local and the scars wrought by the temporary imbalance are soon healed. Because of his mobility and other aspects of his technology, man will be the first species to achieve the swarming stage simultaneously over the whole earth: from the point of view of all the other organisms in all the earth's ecosystems, man is becoming a "pest" everywhere at the same time. Furthermore, as a technological animal, he is more of a pest than other organisms that reach the swarming stage because he uses up nonrenewable resources and produces inorganic by-products, whereas a nontechnological species consumes mainly renewable resources and produces only organic waste.

If *Homo sapiens*, as a reasoning organism, is to have a chance of avoiding the population crash, he must simultaneously, and with the greatest speed, dramatically reduce his consumption of primary mineral material and he must cease to increase his numbers. There cannot be the slightest chance of the former unless the latter is achieved, since recycling any substance with 100 percent efficiency is an impossible goal, and even if achievable, could only cater for the present population at the present level of industrialization.

Three further doublings would produce a world population of 30 billion, and with the kind of birth rates and death
rates experienced in the mid-twentieth century, this could
easily be achieved in less than a century from now. And yet
responsible estimates of the maximum sustained yield of
world food supply have indicated that little more than three
doublings are theoretically possible. It should be noted also
that these estimates assume that all renewable assets are used
with maximum efficiency and that the economic and social
systems of the earth are rigorously managed as a unit with
no major disruptions or mistakes.

Furthermore, the product of this almost inconceivable
feat of organization would be a vast population at a chronic
level of near starvation for the great majority and with personal choice and freedom of action reduced to a level far
below that which obtains at present even in the underpriv-
ileged countries. Nor would there be any possibility what-
soever of any further population increase: those who might
have continued to oppose birth control up to that point
would no longer be able to do so without implicitly con-
demning people to certain death by starvation.

In the face of this prospect it is small wonder that the
final policy statement of the Committee on Resources and
Man of the United States Academy of Sciences contains the
following recommendation:

> That efforts to limit population increase in the nation
> and the world be intensified by whatever means are
> practicable, working towards a goal of zero rate of
> growth by the end of the [twentieth] century.

But even if this demographic miracle can be achieved,
it will only be a short first step. Mere contemplation of the
intricacies of the human ecological problem is depressing
enough, but it is when one begins to consider the measures
that are necessary for a long-term solution that one plumbs
the depths of pessimism. In a world where politicians, econo-

mists, industrialists, and trade unions—capitalist and Communist—are in almost universal agreement that an increased rate of growth is the panacea for nearly all our ills, how can a rapid and complete revolution in thought be possible? When the power of politicians and the wealth of business are ultimately dependent on the number and wealth of constituents and customers, how can it ever be possible to gain voluntary acceptance for a philosophy whose central theme is conservation and contraction?

It is not as though solid economic benefits can be offered as a reward to our children and grandchildren: a contracting economy would, of itself, create problems, and a new race of economists would have to be born to cater for a progressively aging population over two or three generations. In the Western countries in particular it is barely conceivable that any Administration could persuade the population to accept a drastic reduction in standard of living so that conservation policies of worldwide scope could be effected and so that a much larger percentage of resources could be diverted to technology-deficient peoples.

In the present world, dogged by political and economic nationalism, racial tension, and conflicting political and religious ideologies, there seems to be no glimmer of hope that these problems of unprecedented magnitude can be solved in a mere quarter to half a century. It is small wonder that some have already reached the conclusion that *all* optimism is no more than foolish optimism, and that mankind (to use the words of [the American biologist] Paul Ehrlich) may be "too far into the tube already" for any planned solution to be a practical possibility.

Perhaps those who anticipate the end of the road in this way are wrong, and some way out can be found. If so, it can only be through an unimaginable transference of our total scientific effort from exploitation to conservation. It is certainly to be hoped that those who have plumbed the depths of pessimism will not cease to urge constructive action along these lines in order to try to avert what they feel to be almost inevitable.

Tasks for the Planner

Although the problems facing mankind have been presented here as essentially global ones, it should not be inferred that local effort in one's own community is pointless. Politicians must certainly be provided with the information necessary for a global strategy, but this cannot possibly succeed if human ecology on the local scale is not intensively studied to provide a basis for realistic planning. As pressures grow and shortages develop, a constant surveillance of man/ land relationships in all kinds of environments will be a necessity. Indeed the need for analyzing developing land-use problems is so great that the efforts of planners of all kinds should surely not be misdirected and squandered as they are at the present time.

In a situation where so much effort is needed, trained social scientists and technologists must surely forsake many of the purely academic and fruitless exercises to which they are at present devoting their lives. As our cities swell and crumble about our ears, and as our agricultural lands deteriorate and disappear beneath bricks and mortar, it seems incredible that countless academics—be they civil engineers, architects, economists, geographers, or the rest—should sit in their university departments or municipal offices devising theoretical models of cities and transport networks for the year A.D. 2000. There can be no more pointless exercise if the former are to lack the bare necessities of subsistence and the latter are to have no power for traction.

Planning there must certainly be, indeed I am calling for planning at the most fundamental level. But any planning that ignores either of the two fundamentals in the equation—amounts of people and amounts of raw materials —must be baseless. Practitioners of superficial planning are wielding their bows in competition with Nero, and the developing conflagration promises to be a holocaust.

A WORLDWIDE PROBLEM [3]

The Swedes Come Clean

On Sunday a beacon on a hill outside Stockholm will be lit and a warning will be flashed across Sweden by 1,499 other beacons. It is the system once used by the Vikings when invasion threatened. Now the beacons will be lit to dramatize the pollution threat. This will be the high point of Sweden's "Earth Week." The week will also involve state-run exhibitions and demonstrations against pollution; a million students are expected to take part.

Not that the Swedes have the problems that countries such as Britain and Japan have. But 70 percent of their population lives in the cities and the Swedes, with a Nordic passion for cleanliness, do not want to see their environment go the way of others. The contrast is particularly marked with Italy, Japan, and Russia, described in the articles below. Sweden has taken a conscious step away from the Italians, with their Latin laxity about their surroundings, and from the emphasis on economic growth at all costs that marks the Japanese and Russian economies.

Last year [1969] the Swedish parliament enacted a spate of laws restricting pollutants. All DDT insecticides were banned from the beginning of this year; Sweden is the first country to do so. The amount of sulfur—a major pollutant—in oil was limited to 2.5 percent by weight, and this limit is to be further reduced. Stockholm has set itself higher standards by making the sulfur limit 1 percent. A limit has also been set on hydrocarbon in petrol in an attempt to cut down carbon monoxide in city air. To supervise these limits a government body, the National Swedish Nature Conservation Office, has been set up; no other country has such a body.

The government has taken a strong line with industry. The machinery of planning permission is to be used to pre-

[3] From "Pollution: The Swedes Come Clean; Italy: Sewage in Your Eye; Japan: Where It Comes Down in Chunks; Russia: It's No Better Over There." *Economist.* 236:40, 43-4. S. 5, '70. Reprinted by permission.

vent any increase in pollution from industrial waste. A company cannot build a new factory unless it can prove that it will not muck things up. For existing industry, there are government grants to meet 25 percent of the cost of installing antipollution equipment. Industry has no excuse for inaction: a new company, Swedish Waste Conversion, has been formed to market antipollution equipment. And to shake industry into action a time-limit for the cleanup has been set. By 1972 all factories must be in line with the pollution limits, though extensions may be granted to poorer firms.

One interesting idea for meeting the cost of the campaign —a tax on products whose processing causes undue pollution —has been discussed in Sweden. Such a tax would transfer the cost to the consumer, and the tax would vary according to the kind and degree of pollution caused; the idea was that market forces should be used to eradicate a problem for which the demand for industrial goods was largely to blame. But the idea was dropped because of the difficulty of assessing the social cost of pollution in monetary terms.

Swedish public opinion would apparently not object to the introduction of such a tax. In a recent survey 69 percent said they would support an increase in taxes if that meant more money being spent on sewage purification. The press has helped to make people conscious of the danger; every major newspaper has its own pollution correspondent. The universities run pollution courses. There are also government-run evening classes on the techniques of pollution control. Last year 250,000 people passed through these classes, and 10,000 of them went on to take the longer course which enabled them to become pollution officers. Where the Swedes are leading, the rest of the industrial world will sooner or later have to follow.

Italy: Sewage in Your Eye

"The open sewer we insist on calling the Tiber," as one Roman newspaper put it, is off-limits for bathing. Fishing and winkle-picking [snail-gathering] have also been forbidden on the river and on the beaches for 200 meters above and below the river's mouth at Fiumicino. Since municipal politicians are usually loath to interfere with the innocent pleasures of citizens, and rarely like to hurt vested interests, this order given by Rome's mayor this summer created quite a stir. A whole tribe of river folk, the *fiumaroli,* make their living on the Tiber whose pontoon bathing establishments have been landmarks to generations of Romans. At Ostia the mayor's edict struck panic, not so much among the bathers as among the thousands of people who live by the bathing industry along the coast.

Not only the mouth of the Tiber has been declared taboo. The edict applies to dozens of irrigation (and sewage) canals which run into the sea between Anzio, Ostia and Fregene, whose beaches serve 3 million Romans. In fact bathing had been forbidden in such places throughout Italy since 1896, but no one ever took much notice. Now the law which forbids swimming within 200 yards of a sewage outlet is to be strictly enforced.

This rules out a large part of the free beach donated by President Saragat a few years ago out of the presidential estate at Castel Porziano. The gift was intended to save a stretch of beach from the concession-holders who have railed off most of the Mediterranean shore from Genoa to Naples and are charging from 300 to 500 lire a day [50 to 80 cents] for a bathing hut with an umbrella and two deck chairs.

This summer will be remembered in Italy as the year 'of the poisoned sea. In most places pollution is visible to the naked eye and when the sea is calm a wide band of scum hems in all bathers who don't care to get out of their depth. The phenomenon has given a great boost to the rubber canoe business as well as to the producers of more sophisticated craft.

But the big scare really got under way in Genoa, where a brave police magistrate, the praetor, issued the first order forbidding bathing within 200 yards of any sewage canal. Since there are seventy-five such canals in his territory, interspersed by some thirty bathing establishments, the order not unnaturally raised a storm. It was countermanded by another magistrate, and the praetor was severely censured for exceeding his powers. An elegant legal dispute arose on the issue that the praetor—in ignorance of the 1896 law—had based his order on the law forbidding the adulteration of food and drink. The praetor's answer—logical but not legal— is that anyone bathing in the waters of the Ligurian coast is liable to swallow a mouthful of . . . [excrement]. The question is still *sub judice*.

The degree of pollution registered by various institutes up and down the coast is said to be more than a hundred times above the safety level. Curiously, Genoa and Rome outdo Naples. One explanation for this is that industrial pollution in the bay has got the better of the bacteria.

In the south of Italy the problem of pollution has given a new twist to the age-old pattern of intercity strife. Calabria, which has virtually no industry and a low density of population, suffers from the Sicilian habit—practiced by cities as well as by individuals—of disposing of refuse by tying it in plastic bags and hurling these into the sea. The prevailing currents carry these bags across the Straits of Messina to Calabria. The Calabrians are threatening to collect them and hire helicopters to drop them over Messina.

The Italian public is so aware of pollution now that there is hope of the authorities listening to the experts after years of ignoring them. The city authorities in Rome are examining the cost of installing purifying plants at strategic points. The estimate for four plants is some £60 million [about $150 million]. Since Rome's debts are about £1,000 million [$2.4 billion], it is quite clear that the money can never be found without help.

Legislation to deal with pollution languishes in parliament, where draft bills have been presented from time to time by various Socialist ministers. They never got very far. Today it is estimated that 90 percent of Italian industrial companies evade the laws and regulations on pollution.

Signor Mariotti, the minister for health, believes that the
cost of dealing efficiently with pollution is beyond the
strength not merely of municipal finance but of the Italian
state.

Japan: Where It Comes Down in Chunks

No one knows precisely how bad air pollution is in
Tokyo but the findings of research scientists suggest that the
political hullabaloo in Tokyo about pollution has a solid
foundation in fact. Sulfur dioxide concentrations are quite
low compared with other parts of the world, according to
scientists at the Tokyo Institute of Technology, but the levels
of particulate pollution in Japan are between two and four
times higher than those of the United States and Britain. In
addition there are sometimes high concentrations of oxidants in the atmosphere, the scientists say. On July 18 [1970],
oxidants caused twenty-two girls playing handball in Su-
ginami-ku, Tokyo, to collapse in heaps.

Generally speaking the "particulates" are the villains of
the piece in Tokyo: solids and liquids suspended in mid-air,
chunks of dirt, acid "mists," sulfates, nitrates and metals.
These are the things which leave a distinct stain on the collar
in half a day and smudge curtains almost as rapidly. They
have been steadily reduced in London over the past fifteen
years, but not in Tokyo, which still has no proper regulations to control them (it checks only sulfur dioxide).

The problem for Tokyo, and for Osaka, is that there are
concentrations of heavy industry both in the city and close
by—at Kawasaki, for instance, which lies between Tokyo and
Yokohama. When the winds blow in the wrong direction
Tokyo receives waste products from Kawasaki chimneys on
top of the pollution from motor traffic in the Tokyo area.
Under their combined effect high buildings gradually blur
or disappear behind a whitish veil and a haze hangs over
traffic crossings. Oxygen-vending machines have even been
installed in some of Tokyo's foulest streets so that passers-by
can recharge themselves with a gulp of pure oxygen.

The Tokyo authorities have responded by starting a warning system against the photochemical smog which is created by the action of bright sunlight on certain gases. The system came into effect [in 1970], and warnings have frequently been given since. But the only recommended escape is to "go indoors and rest."

The national government has also started to move. At the end of July [1970] an antipollution headquarters was opened in the prime minister's office, and senior ministers have decided that new pollution legislation will be necessary. The government has also announced paper plans for "eliminating" pollution in the big cities by 1980, and for stopping the use of lead compounds in petrol; it has also announced new regulations against dumping muck in rivers. The finance ministry has said that the public should not shoulder the whole cost of pollution control. Business must be made to pay its share.

It has all come a little late. The opposition parties say that the ruling Liberal-Democrats have concentrated on economic growth no matter what, and been soft on big business firms which contribute to their funds. Whether these things are so or not the Japanese public has found a new issue with which to chastise the government. Even extremists in the student Zengakuren movement took up pollution at their annual conference this summer. For them it was "a symbol of Japanese imperialism."

In May [1970] there was a national outcry that the victims of the "Minimata disease" had been awarded so little compensation by the Japanese courts. The illness—named after the town of Minimata where the victims mostly live—was caused by the eating of fish taken from water polluted by mercury waste from a certain factory. The outcry has been loud partly because the mercury poisoning killed about 45 people, with 71 survivors left in poor health, and partly because it has taken ten years to reach a compensation settlement. As one newspaper, the *Mainichi Shimbun,* said, noting that the compensation for thalidomide cases in

Britain had been five times the amount paid to the Minimata victims: "Why must the life of a Japanese be worth a fifth of that of an Englishman?"

In general, Japanese companies have been none too careful about how they dispose of effluents, mainly because the Japanese have not been fully aware of the dangers until quite recently. But now reports of any new pollution sickness receive great publicity. The days when industry could get away with it are over.

Russia: It's No Better Over There

Because the Soviet Union is not a capitalist country it is often thought that there must be less pollution there. Pollution in the West is usually blamed on an economic system which takes no account of the cost of pollution to society in general. Yet it seems that the Soviet Union is as bad as we are.

Most Russian cities have a high level of carbon monoxide in the air—though there are few cars by Western standards. The trouble is the impure Russian petrol. Very few factories have air-purifying devices. Water pollution by oil, sewage and industrial waste is worse: it is said to be costing . . . [approximately $7.2 billion] a year. The yield of fish from rivers, lakes and seas has dropped sharply and, most serious of all, the catch of sturgeon—and so of caviar—has been badly affected. There is even talk of making artificial caviar. Reckless forest clearing threatens to create dustbowls on the American-prairie scale. And pulp mills are in the process of destroying Lake Baikal's claim to be the world's largest body of fresh water.

For such a sparsely populated country the situation is needlessly bad. Not that official efforts are not being made. There are pollution limits, and a watchdog committee exists in the body known as the Ministry of Amelioration and Irrigation Systems. The official papers, *Pravda* and *Izvestia,* have come out in favor of pollution control. Even Russia's dissenters have turned their attention to the problem; Professor

[Andrei] Sakharov devoted part of his recent clandestinely published criticism of Soviet policy to the danger.

But the damage was done before officialdom became pollution-conscious. Not long ago conservationists in the Soviet Union laid themselves open to the charge of trying to sabotage production targets. Now they are freer to object. But there remains the obstacle to reform caused by the nature of the Soviet system itself.

All sectors of industry have production targets to meet. Managers who find that their factory has fallen below its target cannot afford pollution control because it may limit output as well as cost a lot of money. *Izvestia* recently complained that the attitude of most managers was, "We deliver the goods and the rest is of no importance." Another difficulty is caused by the Marxist theory of value, which holds that value is created by labor and therefore regards unworked raw materials as free. This has led to a highly wasteful exploitation of resources. For example, 75,000 acres are wasted each year by open-cast mining. If interest were charged on the capital used for the job the mining firms might concentrate more on deep-shaft mining to get their money's worth.

The central government provides funds to help industries meet the cost of pollution control. But they are small. The drive to catch up with the West in terms of production has meant an unwillingness to spend on nonproductive projects like purification filters. And there is evidence that much of these funds is misspent. Last year *Pravda* accused one factory manager of using such funds to meet his production quota; the case is probably typical of many. Misuse of these funds is made easier by the fact that they are not allocated for specific projects but are included, in a lump sum, in the budget of each ministry. But each ministry has an overall production target and it often needs everything it can lay its hands on to meet this. The Ministry of Chemical Industry, whose factories are among the worst polluters, is said to be particularly prone to this.

Penalties are being made tougher and commensurate with the damage done. Two senior officials of an Estonian cellulose plant were recently fined the equivalent of £900 [$2,160] each, had 10 percent cuts in their pay and were placed on probation for polluting a fish hatchery. But it is unlikely that any real good will be done until antipollution funds are used for their proper purpose.

IMPERILED AFRICA [4]

Along Kenya's Tana River, Pokomo tribesmen relax under palm-thatched sunshades and unwittingly watch some of East Africa's future slip away to the sea.

While they guard against crop-eating animals, land-eating erosion from slash-and-burn farming muddies the Tana so you can't see your hand a few centimeters below the surface. Clothes washed in that water show a brown tinge for weeks thereafter.

Wildlife enthusiasts rarely mention this dimension of habitat destruction when charting the fate of East Africa's mammals. Yet, as [the late] noted paleontologist Louis S. B. Leakey points out, man himself probably is the most endangered species.

His encroachments on the living space of lions, elephants, and antelopes are destroying his own essential environment as he enlarges the range of poor land-management.

Discussing this before the American Association for the Advancement of Science last Christmas [1971], Dr. Leakey added that such land destruction is not inevitable.

"The Intelligence to Learn"

"Men," he said, "do have the intelligence to learn from their environmental mistakes. Unlike the dinosaurs, they do have the capacity to manage their environment successfully."

[4] From "What Is Man Doing to East Africa?" by Robert C. Cowen, staff correspondent. Christian Science Monitor. p 7. My. 31, '72. Reprinted by permission from The Christian Science Monitor. © 1972. The Christian Science Publishing Society. All rights reserved.

Here, then, is the real ecological challenge East Africa faces.

To see it merely in terms of man vs. game animals, as is so often done, misses its main thrust. To prosper in this harsh yet fragile environment, to develop modern economies, East Africans must so understand and manage their land that both men and animals can survive.

Dr. Kai Curry-Lindahl, United Nations regional expert in ecology and conservation, says that African leaders are beginning to realize that the success of their cherished plans for industrialization turn on this point. Wherever he goes throughout Africa, he says he finds the essential natural-resource base for such industrial development threatened.

He explains that North America and Western Europe have massive environmental problems. But these have come as the result of industrialization, including industrialization of farming. In the first place, they had a base of natural resources from which to develop their industrial prosperity.

But in Africa, he now finds poor land-use eroding that base before industrial development has scarcely begun. It especially threatens the semiarid East African lands, because they easily could become deserts.

"Bad land-use is destroying the remarkable resource background needed for development here," he says. "Deserts and dry savanna continue to encroach. Former perennial watercourses now are dry for long periods."

I know what he means. A series of "permanent" water holes near one camp we visited had dried up.

Mountain forests, the water-catchment areas of the region, are going. In Dr. Curry-Lindahl's judgment, all remaining such forests have more economic value as accumulators and regulators of the water supply than they do as timber reserves.

Replanting them to quick-growing species such as eucalyptus is no substitute for leaving them in their natural state. These stands of commercial species just are not good enough as water managers.

Fire, too, is taking an increasing toll. Dr. Curry-Lindahl calls it a useful land-management tool—in its place. "But," he says, "used indiscriminately to clear land for primitive farming or cattle grazing, it's 95 percent bad. It kills soil organisms, let alone doing other damage."

And everywhere you go in East Africa, you are likely to see one or more smoke columns on the horizon.

Thoughtless timber cutting, slash-and-burn farming, and firing grasslands for pasture have gone on for centuries. Many ecologists believe they helped create the deserts to the north of Kenya. But now, with population booming, the uncontrolled spread of such practices directly threatens the whole of East Africa.

What is hopeful about this challenge, Dr. Curry-Lindahl says, is that both ecologists and political leaders are waking up to this menace while there's still time to avert it. However, he admits that developing sound land-management will be an uphill fight and that the next one to two decades will be crucial.

Man—Most Neglected Factor

Even scientists concerned mainly with game parks and their magnificent animals are coming to realize that man is the most important—and neglected—single factor in their ecological studies.

At Tanzania's famed Serengeti National Park, a handful of specialists working at the Serengeti Research Institute (SRI) have sketched at least the broad outlines of this environmental picture. Dr. Hugh Lamprey describes it as a finely tuned system responding to the rhythm of Africa's general climate in which every animal, plant, and insect has a special place.

The basic rhythm seems to be a roughly eleven-year swing between cycles of drought and good rainfall. SRI scientists expect 1972 to 1980 to be dry.

While there are many local variations within this general pattern, Dr. Lamprey says the productivity of grass and other basic food plants keeps pace, species by species, area by area, with the rainfall rhythm. And all animal life then is keyed to that productivity.

Within this system, each animal species uses a particular food supply, generally not competing with others. Some species may even prepare a food resource for other animals. Thus wildebeests eat long grass down to a length that just suits gazelles.

Overall, the supply of food, reflecting rainfall, regulates animal numbers. There are wide swings in population. Serengeti's vast wildebeest herds, for example, seem to build up toward a million individuals only to crash back to a few hundred thousand.

But with lions and other predators regulating the magnitude of such population swings, Dr. Lamprey says it has become clear that no one species either grows to the point of habitat destruction or dies out completely.

In the past, men were a natural part of this living system. Now, Dr. Lamprey notes, men have set themselves apart from it.

Within the great game parks they are totally excluded except as visitor-observers. No one knows what change their absence as part of the natural community is bringing.

Intense tourist observing does seem to distress some of the animals, altering their behavior. Lions, for example, are often interrupted when trying to hunt. And some animals, such as nesting ostriches, are sometimes so disturbed they abandon nests or young.

Meanwhile, outside the parks, man is becoming the only member of a once well-adjusted living system to reach the point of serious habitat destruction.

You can sense just how sensitive this fragile environment is from the destruction caused within the game parks by vehicle tracks. The second minibus or four-wheel drive to go down a track probably reduces the productivity of that bit of grassland by 50 percent, Dr. Lamprey estimates. A few more passes, and the track becomes a more or less permanent scar.

Dr. Lamprey says the number of tracks has grown 250 percent in the past three years. He expects it will rise another 300 percent by 1975.

Vehicles are a major grassland destroyer which he feels must be regulated. He admits, though, that he doesn't know how the parks can persuade tour operators to stay on established roads and not "go visit the lions."

Fragility Emphasized

The track problem emphasizes the fragility of East Africa's environment. Dr. Lamprey thinks scientists urgently need to understand men's ecological role here both for good park-management and safe development outside the parks. Unknowledgeable settlement and farming merely for settlement's sake could easily destroy the land people are trying to develop.

Unfortunately, such studies are politically sensitive and, hence, unpopular. "Anthropologists aren't very welcome here these days," Dr. Lamprey observes.

In Kenya, National Parks director Perez Olindo puts the matter bluntly. He warns readers outside Africa not to be misled by reports of pressures for more farmland. Generally, he says, such pressures come from ignorance rather than real agricultural need.

Destroy the vegetation, put in seed, hope to get fruit—this is the biggest fallacy I know [he says]. It is a good way to make desert. The arable lands we now cultivate are not properly used. They are farmed on a subsistence basis.

We respect the presidential slogan "back to the land." But sending back people who know nothing about the land, its capability and limits, would be foolhardy. The solution is to establish small institutes of agriculture. Then when a person has graduated and knows how to manage he would be given land.

There is no real need even to think of encroaching on the game parks to get farmland until we have done all we can with the farmland we already have.

Often wildlife make the best use of the land even when you think of what advantage agriculture might do. Silt-laden river water can be bad for irrigation. It can spread waterborne disease. Such irrigation requires major capital investment. Why go to that extent when wildlife [Kenya's second biggest foreign-exchange earner after coffee] is already earning a good return without such investment?

It is both the soil and wildlife which we must manage properly. It is a matter of intelligent management and economic returns, not a sentimental conflict of interests between men and animals. This idea is moving ahead.

In Africa, we can learn from environmental mistakes of other regions. It is one reason why we can move ahead fast. That is why I am not discouraged in spite of formidable problems national parks here face.

Easy to Be Discouraged

Certainly, an outsider could be discouraged by some of these problems.

In Tanzania, a local official has allowed a tribe to settle on one hundred square miles of Serengeti parkland which could be important in the wildebeest's seasonal migrations. At this writing, no one knows whether the central government will reverse this decision. It came against a background of uncertainty over vaguely defined governmental plans to generally settle the areas around the park.

In Kenya, the government wants to make Mr. Olindo's now independent agency a government department. This could subject good park-management to political influences.

A visitor can't meaningfully assess such involved local issues during a brief tour. Yet even a quick glimpse at least suggests that such problems should not sway one's perspective, important though the problems may temporarily be.

Political maneuvering, conflicts of interest, selfishness have always arisen when people developed their lands. Here these compete with a growing awareness that sound environmental management is essential for the well-being of men as well as animals.

Such awareness was missing when Europe and America made their environmental mess. Its presence as a political factor can make all the difference.

That, Mr. Olindo says, is why he is so confident that East Africa has a hopeful future.

II. IN DEFENSE OF PROGRESS
AND TECHNOLOGY

EDITOR'S INTRODUCTION

"We have heard of nothing but decay," the British historian Lord Macaulay once remarked. "We have seen nothing but progress." Such, indeed, is the theme struck by the articles in this section. Like the poor, the prophets of gloom and doom seem always to be with us. And it may be, as Norman Podhoretz intimates in the first article, that intellectuals have a particular weakness for visions of cosmic destruction. As Podhoretz maintains, however, there may also be little evidence in modern life to support their gloomy prognoses. It was only a few years ago that the doom-sayers were wringing their hands over the threat of nuclear war. That threat having diminished, have they merely found new avenues for the dissemination of their dire message?

Almost two centuries ago, the same arguments that are now being put forward by ecological pessimists were being propounded by Thomas Malthus, whose theories have been challenged in the intervening years. Far from the brink of progressive starvation that Malthus foresaw, man has now reached the point at which, for the first time in history and with the help of modern science and technology, starvation and disease are being vigorously and often successfully combated in all parts of the globe. As the authors in this section see it, moreover, the advances that have brought a more abundant food supply and a prolonged life span can also be expected to yield results when applied to the problems of environmental deterioration. With the help of technicians, polluted rivers have been made to run clean and shores unsafe for swimming have been restored. Even now the air in many of our major cities is improving in quality, given the effective combination of popular concern and technical expertise.

Beyond these considerations, however, there is the problem of the damage done to public perceptions by exaggerated claims of environmental disaster. For one thing, such claims can dull the public's receptivity to genuinely serious environmental problems requiring immediate attention. For another, they can tempt the public into false or counterproductive solutions. The conviction that economic growth is an outworn concept, for example, could literally condemn hundreds of millions who now live in poverty to a future without hope.

The articles in this section advocate the case for progress and technology, but they also of necessity address themselves to the arguments of the pessimists, such as Eyre, whose views are expressed in Section I. After Podhoretz's dismissal of the most exaggerated of these claims, the president of the National Academy of Sciences, Philip Handler, makes a plea for cautious optimism in the treatment of ecological crises or alarms. Next, a research scientist for Standard Oil Company of Ohio sets out to debunk the idea that only drastic solutions can win the environmental cause and warns the public that crying wolf can become a dangerous game. Finally, an expert with the United States Forest Service gives his own critical appraisal of what's right—and wrong—with the environmental movement today.

THE PROPHETS OF DOOM AND GLOOM [1]

For . . . [one] strain of apocalyptic thinking which has been gathering force and influence in the last few years, . . . the human species has reached a point at which it is about to destroy itself altogether and quite possibly the entire planet as well. The contemporary avatar of this ancient expectation of an imminent End of Days was given a powerful

[1] From "Doomsday Fears & Modern Life," by Norman Podhoretz, editor. Commentary. 52:4+. O. '71. Reprinted from Commentary, by permission; Copyright © 1971 by the American Jewish Committee.

stimulus by the invention of nuclear weapons, and if not for one of the most curious and least remarked developments of the curious age in which we live, it might well have gone on indefinitely looking to the mushroom cloud for the perverse comfort a great anxiety always finds in the thought that its fears are real. The curious development was that everyone suddenly stopped believing in the possibility of a major nuclear war.

When exactly, this astonishing change occurred, or why it should have occurred at all, would be very hard to say; conceivably it was an effect of the Cuban missile crisis. But whatever the reasons may be, there is no question that very few people still seriously fear the eruption of a major nuclear war between the United States and the Soviet Union or for that matter between the United States and China—the kind of war that used to be associated with visions of the end of the world and that was so recently considered by so many to be a virtual inevitability. It is true that the idea of a limited nuclear war between Israel and Egypt or even between the Soviet Union and China still seems plausible, but such a war, whether rightly or wrongly, is no longer commonly imagined to spell the end of the world.

The fascinating consequence is that we rarely find any great emphasis being put on nuclear war nowadays by the catastrophist schools of apocalyptic thought. They mention it, of course, they trot it out and bow to it and pay it their obeisance. But they do so in a spirit of perfunctory piety which perfectly expresses their recognition that it has all at once become a doddering presence in the contemporary imagination, that it has lost its power to convince. For the moment at least, that power has passed to pollution. Technology is destroying ecology and will end by destroying us all: so, stated in the most general terms, runs the formula which in not much more than a year or two has won a most amazing degree of uncritical acceptance in every circle and on every side.

Thus ideas which only yesterday would have been dismissed as crackpot are today given a respectful hearing. There is, for example, the theory that thermal pollution is melting the polar ice cap by slow but inexorable degrees, so that the end of the world will come by flood (in direct contravention of the biblical promise expressed in the symbol of the rainbow). Or, on the contrary, we are told that the rays of the sun are being effectively blocked by the pollution of the air, so that the end of the world will come by frost. More plausibly E. J. Mishan, a catastrophist who has nothing whatever of the crackpot in him, warns of "the chances of extinction of our species from uncontrolled epidemics caused by the deadlier viruses that have evolved in response to widespread application of new 'miracle' drugs, or from some ecological calamity caused by our inadvertent destruction of those forms of animal and insect life that once preyed on the pests that consumed men's harvests." [For a further discussion of Professor Mishan's views, see "The Curse of the GNP," in Section III below.—Ed.]

"Repent, for the End Is Near!"

Professor Mishan, unlike some others among us of an apocalyptic bent of mind, is well aware that "the belief that the end of the world was drawing nigh has been widely held at different times in human history." But he will allow no consolation to be gained from this, for the "doomsday fears of yesterday had no rational basis" while "those of today have plenty." This seems to me an amazingly arrogant statement, especially coming from a writer who professes in other contexts to have so little faith in the superiority of the modern understanding of the mysteries of life on this planet to the wisdoms of "yesterday." The truth is that the doomsday fears of today have as much or as little rational basis as doomsday fears ever did, if by rational we mean subject to scientific proof. No proof exists that the end of the world is at hand. We do not even have persuasive evidence pointing

to that conclusion. All we have, exactly as the men of yesterday did, are warnings and exhortations to the effect that we
are doomed unless we repent and change our ways and return to the proper path. That such warnings and exhortations are often voiced by professional scientists and couched
in the language of science does not in the least endow them
with the authority of tested scientific statements. When they
speak of these matters, the scientists in quesion are speaking
not as scientists but as moralists and ideologues, and no one
ought to be fooled.

But if there is no rational basis for the apocalypticism of
Mishan and others, neither is Sir Peter Medawar right on
the other side in asserting that "the deterioration of the environment produced by technology is a technological problem for which technology has found, is finding, and will
continue to find solutions." Even setting aside the interesting
theoretical question of how a problem which is by definition
a consequence of the growth of technology can be solved by
the further growth of technology, one must still reject the
notion—so characteristic of a certain type of liberal men-
tality—that anything can be had for nothing provided the
right formula or gimmick or gadget can be found. Surely
where the benefits of technology are concerned, as with human affairs in all of their many modalities, there will always
be a price to pay, and the price will always be high, and
justly high in the case of technology considering what it can
buy. The air of industrial societies will never be as sweet as
the air of a mountain retreat; cities will never afford the
"margin, space, ease and openness" for which critics like
Mishan so eloquently yearn, however lacking in eloquence
and however philistine the spirit in which they speak of the
gains in freedom of every kind—from want, from disease,
from tribal coercion, from claustrophobia—that are purchased, most willingly and eagerly by most people the minute
they are given the chance, through the sacrifice of other un-
doubted goods to the gods of advanced modernity.

The Trouble With Doomsayers

In saying that there will always be a price for technology, and that the price will always be high, I do not by any means wish to suggest that it cannot be lowered to some extent or that technology itself cannot be employed to that end. For it is undoubtedly true that some of the dangerous and unpleasant consequences of technology can be softened or even eliminated by technological means. Ways can be found of producing energy that are less damaging to the environment than traditional methods have been (though there is always the likelihood that these new methods will take their toll of different features of the environment than present methods do). Factories and automobiles and airplanes can in fact be equipped with devices—technological devices—that cut down on the volume of noxious material they pour into the atmosphere; streams and rivers already polluted can in fact be cleaned up and the air can be cleaned up too (though there is always the likelihood that all this can only be accomplished at the expense of other social and even ecological goods). Nevertheless, as much of this kind of thing as can be done should be done, just as at an earlier stage of industrial development certain necessary measures were taken in the field of sanitation and in the field of public health.

It is precisely here that the damaging effects of the apocalyptic perspective make themselves most vividly felt. On the issue of the environment, as on so many other issues, the prophets of doom are often excused or even praised on the ground that they "wake people up" to the existence of a problem and therefore contribute to the mobilization of the political will necessary to work toward solutions. My own observation is that, on the contrary, prophecies of doom are more likely to put people to sleep than to wake them up: why bother striving if the end is in sight? And when it is not serving to induce apathy, the apocalyptic perspective is serving to prepare for and justify the institution of extraordinary measures of political control. For to announce the apocalypse is, at bottom, to declare a state of emergency, and the suspension of normal liberties is one of the first things that happens when a state of emergency is declared. On this account alone, if for no other reason, any alarmist or catastrophist view of any public problem—especially one so fundamental as the survival of the species itself—ought to be received with the greatest skepticism, and the heaviest burden of proof put on anyone who wishes to persuade us that we are doomed unless we radically change our ways. In the face of the clear eagerness of the vast majority of people—not just in the Western countries, but everywhere, all over the world —to acquire or hold on to the benefits of life in an advanced industrial society, and in the face of their obvious willingness to pay even an exorbitant price, only the most extreme measures of political, social, and moral coercion could accomplish the kind of reversal of the forces of technological growth which the apocalyptic critics tell us is our only alternative to doom.

For myself I believe in the existence of a third alternative which is to accept modern society, with its imperatives of restless growth, as a *viable* human possibility superior to some the world has seen and inferior to others but in any case a viable possibility and a *natural* one: a poor thing, perhaps, but our own. It is the way into which *we* were born and the way in which we are going to die, and it is the way in which, between those two points, we have to make a life. To make a life is to strike a continuing series of bargains— with nature, with the past, with the future—and to make a good life is to make the soundest and fairest bargains we can. This is not what the apocalyptic perspective asks us or encourages us to do, but it is the best we can do and it probably is all we should ever even try.

EXAGGERATION: THE OTHER
POLLUTION PERIL [2]

If you've been concerned by claims that pollution immediately imperils our environment, you'll be interested in the views of Dr. Philip Handler, president of the National Academy of Sciences.

In this interview with *Nation's Business*, Dr. Handler contends that while pollution problems are indeed grave, they may well be less acute than they so frequently are made out to be. And he cites a danger of emotional overreaction which he says can lead to insufficiently considered controls.

He feels we have the time for proper research which will enable us to enact reasonable antipollution laws to protect the environment without unnecessarily endangering the economy.

The privately endowed Academy which Dr. Handler heads is the nation's most distinguished organization of scientists. . . .

Since his election in 1969 to a six-year term as head of the Academy, he has gained a reputation for speaking out.

He has strongly criticized the Administration on some aspects of Federal spending for science, and on occasion has opposed prevailing opinion in the scientific community—as he does here on some important pollution questions.

Dr. Handler, you are one of the few scientists who say environmental pollution problems are being exaggerated. Yet many of your colleagues contend the pollution situation has reached the danger point. If the experts disagree, where does this leave average citizens?

Well, I hope it leaves them open-minded, willing to look about themselves and willing to read.

The evidence of environmental deterioration is all too evident and there are local instances where the damage is

[2] From interview with Dr. Philip Handler, biochemist and president of the National Academy of Sciences. *Nation's Business.* 59:30-3. Ap. '71. © 1971, Nation's Business—the Chamber of Commerce of the United States. Reprinted by permission.

beyond tolerance and perhaps dangerous to man. I don't differ from my colleagues with regard to the long-term seriousness of these problems. But I also view them as varying widely in the magnitude and urgency of the threat to man.

I wish to avoid undertaking supposedly mitigating measures which generate new and even less understood problems. The basic problems are severe enough without unnecessary exaggeration.

Finding lead or mercury in modest amounts in some foodstuff is trouble enough without hysteria. Contending with the consequences of an excess of an old friend like phosphate in detergents should not be relieved by substituting a new devil of unknown properties.

Could you give examples of exaggerated claims about pollution?

Probably the best known is Lake Erie. Erie is surely filthy around its periphery. But the center of the lake is not a "dying body of water" as has been claimed.

The amount of fish protein taken from the lake by commercial fisheries last year was close to the all-time high. They weren't catching the same species as in the past. The game fish that used to be at the top of the food chain are not thriving now; fish below them on the food ladder now dominate. But they are quite adequate for many purposes, so the commercial fishermen take them.

A lake producing all that protein cannot be called dead, and surely affords the opportunity to reverse the damage.

Lake Washington, near Seattle, was called a dying body of water a few years ago. By dint of enormous political effort the situation was turned around; that is, the amount of untreated sewage going into the lake was markedly reduced.

Since this happened, I am told, the lake has difficulty in supporting salmon, the game fish that was at the top of the food ladder. Smaller fish have taken over, much as in Lake Erie, but for quite different reasons.

Please understand that no one in his right mind would favor going back to polluting Lake Washington. My point is that ecosystems are very complex; some are very fragile, others self-sustaining. Any steps that the Government takes in the public interest must first be carefully weighed for all possible consequences.

Despite our pollution, our public health is excellent by historic standards. The world was less hygienic through most of history than it is now. The behavior of the citizens of London and Paris until the last century would offend any American today. They had open sewers in the streets and thought nothing of tossing slops out of windows.

We have come a long way since, but we now may desire a cleaner environment than we can afford in view of our other aspirations—perhaps even cleaner than necessary.

You believe then, that management of the environment involves a series of either/or questions? For example, that society either accepts some pollution from power plants, or there won't be enough electrical power to maintain the present standard of living?

Exactly. The world has to be viewed through realistic glasses. In managing the environment, we must learn to make judgments by weighing risks versus benefits.

Do scientists and the Government lack the knowledge to set antipollution standards and to regulate the quality of the environment?

Yes and no. There are serious holes in our knowledge of the mechanisms and effects of many types of pollution. It will take coordinated research efforts in the laboratory and in the field to obtain the data needed to establish truly appropriate regulations concerning pollution.

An indication of what is needed was provided by a recent National Academy of Sciences and National Academy of Engineering study, which estimated that around 2,600 man-years would be required to take a reasonable first step in understanding the basis for waste management in coastal regions.

This really isn't a huge effort: only about five hundred men for about five years. Other programs would be needed in other areas.

When the new Environmental Protection Agency, the Council for Environmental Quality and the National Oceanic and Atmospheric Administration have grown into their jobs, such programs will become imperative to them. And they will seem rather cheap.

If it will take several years to establish realistic antipollution regulations, how should we proceed in the immediate future?

We need time to acquire the understanding upon which to base such regulations. Meanwhile there are obvious excesses and enough understanding for this go-round of regulation. I'm not sure how much time is required to design or install the necessary technology.

As we repair old wrongs, presumably industry must bear the costs of undoing its own polluting. But that must be done fairly, enforced equitably across the country. Within the United States no company should be given a competitive edge by penalizing its rivals.

It isn't quite so clear how to proceed when we want domestic concerns to avoid polluting while their international competitors proceed unchecked.

In any case, current understanding will undoubtedly suffice to permit reasonable and wise decisions with respect to most major environmental problems.

Which types of pollution do you consider most serious? Do you have a priority list?

No, I don't have one that is carefully worked out.

Probably the matter of primary importance is assurance of an abundant water supply of high quality. We cannot exaggerate our requirement for a healthful, clean water supply.

How big a job is it going to be to straighten out the most serious water pollution problems?

It is a huge, expensive but probably feasible task. A large fraction of our supply comes from major rivers and lakes—water that we necessarily use over and over again. Going back to Lake Erie, the edges are badly polluted. But the task of cleaning it up isn't impossible.

Apparently, this is also true of most of our great rivers. The Mississippi still is bearing fish throughout most of its length. Rivers like the Hudson are difficult but not hopeless.

My point is to sound a note of hope. A great deal can be accomplished by utilizing current technology to stop the most serious sources of pollution.

What is next on your priority list?

Air. We cannot exaggerate our requirement for a healthful, clean air supply.

But I am not aware of any large, heavily populated area in the United States which is in acute trouble for its air supply. The exception is the occasional temperature inversion, when the air essentially becomes stagnant and the concentration of undesirable gases and particulates rises seriously.

The automobile exhaust emission problem can be managed in a few years, probably. Technologies will surely be developed for abatement of the undesirable visible and invisible exhausts of industrial smokestacks.

By now you gather that I do not underestimate the magnitude or seriousness of these problems. What I wish also to convey is that we yet have the time, and already have much of the technology, to manage them; that the way to a better tomorrow is more, not less technology.

How does the pesticide problem rate on your priority list?

I may get myself in trouble with my constituency but I find the stress with respect to pesticides exaggerated.

I join my nature-loving friends in their concern for the handful of bird species that seem to be endangered. But the alternatives, at the moment, are even worse. To do without available pesticides, the price to man would be too high.

We have no choice but to learn how to use the pesticides we have—to use them sparingly and wisely, rather than foolishly abolishing them entirely.

Will it be possible to develop new classes of pesticides?

Yes, I very much hope so. We hope to learn how to operate biological control systems. That is, use natural attractants to collect specific species of undesirable insects and then destroy them or render them infertile.

Haven't such systems already been started?

It has been done for a few species. There is no theoretical reason why we couldn't extend the list. In the end, if we can do that with key pests, we can protect our crops and health, and avoid doing damage by an excess of pesticides. Hopefully such procedures will not lead to some other, presently unpredicted, catastrophe.

At the moment we have succumbed to the pressure to ban DDT. We have placed on the market what is called the second generation of pesticides, which work on a quite different principle. These are the compounds like malathion and parathion. Unlike DDT, they are highly toxic to man; they blinded and even killed numbers of people in 1970. I hope we can avoid such tragedy in 1971.

You said earlier that you hope the average citizen will keep up to date on pollution information. Should he also take an active part in deciding what antipollution regulations the nation actually needs?

Yes. But the process is necessarily complex. Only an informed citizenry will vote the bonds necessary to improve sewage disposal systems or water supplies; will accept the higher costs of almost everything that will come from the wide variety of effort required if the environment is to be protected as so many demand.

But I hope they will not vote to return to "good old days" that never were.

Are you thinking of a vote in which the entire population participates—a referendum?

In some instances we could have a referendum. In general I would rather use the classical technique of electing wise men to public office and abiding by their decisions. By and large they have shown greater wisdom than have referenda.

It is also evident that we are to learn to live with class suits, with citizens' challenges to government action, etc. Indeed, the history of the use of Section 102 of the Environmental Policy Act, which makes such challenges possible, will be a fascinating chapter in our national life.

How do you evaluate the President's recent State of the Environment Message [see *Weekly Compilation of Presidential Documents,* February 15, 1971] *and his recommendations for antipollution laws?*

Those were well-considered and, in my view, in the right direction, but I don't think it is for me to comment on the legal mechanics.

A joint report by the National League of Cities and the United States Conference of Mayors says $37 billion may be needed over six years to completely modernize sewage and waste water facilities. Do you have any cost estimates?

I have yet another number in mind. I can't guarantee its validity, but I've heard repeatedly that it would take about 15 percent of the gross national product to clean up the environment in all its aspects and then to continue to protect it from pollution. In today's economy that would amount to an annual $150 billion, a sizable sum. And this investment would have to continue on a sustained basis.

This would be a 15 percent add-on cost and would be at the expense of the GNP. There would be fewer goods and services to go around for the same level of effort.

But this investment would be a major new source of jobs. Another offsetting advantage would be a decline in the social costs of environmental deterioration, a real enough phenomenon but difficult to manage in the national accounts.

Will the recycling of solid wastes ever be important commercially?

It simply must become commercially attractive. Either that or our standard of living is going to decline.

We have to make recycling work on two counts. First, we must find an acceptable method of disposing of this enormous amount of solid waste. We speak of our society as a high consumption society, but we don't really consume. We pass everything through. And then we have to find some place to unload it.

The second reason is the variety of materials which sooner or later will be in short supply. We have no choice but to reuse them. Applicable processes now exist for some. It is a matter of installing plants and being willing to pay for the increased cost of materials. But we must not slowly convert the oceans into a dilute solution of our rarest metals.

Has pollution of the oceans become a real problem?

The National Academy of Sciences recently reported pesticides are beginning to build up in the oceans. Not in amounts which are cause for alarm, but this is the kind of thing we must keep tabs on.

It is hard to believe we have contaminated the oceans, since such vast quantities of pollutants are required. But we need to admit the possibility.

At this point, I don't think there is any single pollutant in the deep oceans that we need to worry about although there may be problems along the continental coasts.

Is the danger from oil spills as great as it's sometimes made out to be?

During World War II, more than fifty tankers were sunk off Florida's east coast in a two-year period; the beaches were covered with oil, and it backed up in shallow waters. Yet sea life thrives there normally.

Nobody advocates oil spills, of course, but I think the resiliency, the ability of nature to repair itself, is greater than some environmentalists seem to feel.

How would you summarize the pollution situation?

Those who, in my view, exaggerate the nature or magnitude of the pollution problem nevertheless are on the side of the angels. They want a clean, healthy United States. To argue with that is nonsense. And they have generated a climate in which effective action should be possible.

Our problems are to accurately assess environmental hazards, learn the processes which are involved, and reach realistic public decisions about their management.

Public panic is as completely unwarranted as concern is justified.

CRYING "WOLF" SOLVES NOTHING [3]

For several years I have been deeply concerned about reports of the destruction of our environment as a result of technological recklessness, overpopulation and a religious and philosophical outlook that gives little consideration to the preservation of nature. My studies in this area of concern have turned up evidence that I feel compelled to share with you. I welcome this opportunity to do it.

I find that many people I talk to are filled with gloom and believe we have no future. Some of them blame our apparent demise on the Judeo-Christian ethic that it is God's will that man exploit nature for his proper ends and that we have overdone it. Others recommend that we return 2,500 years and embrace the practices of druidism. Many express a disdain for science and mistrust technology in general.

[3] From "A Question of Ecology: The Cries of Wolf," address by Dr. A. L. Jones, research scientist at Standard Oil of Ohio, delivered to the Public Relations Society of America, Greater Cleveland chapter, Hotel Statler Hilton, Cleveland, Ohio, December 14, 1971. *Vital Speeches of the Day.* 38:381-4. Ap. 1, '72. Reprinted by permission.

Our automobiles are no longer a wondrous method of freeing man from his immobility but instead have become terrible polluters and ultimately piles of junk to desecrate the landscape. Electricity, which has been the most convenient form of energy ever available, has come into disrepute. The industry that produces it is looked upon as an evil organization of the Establishment whose objective is to create new radiation hazards with atomic plants, cut down trees, stick poles in the ground and pump smoke into the air to poison all of us.

Many believe we are seriously depleting the oxygen of the atmosphere and replacing it with toxic substances such as carbon monoxide. Some say that Lake Erie is dead and all of us will be next. It is a gloomy picture being painted. This outlook is not justified by the evidence I have been able to find. This is what I want to talk to you about.

I wish to make it quite clear that I am speaking to you as a scientist and not as an emotional supporter of any particular "side" of ecology. I would like to remind you that useful science is based on reproducible evidence or principles that can be repeated and verified by others. As scientists we must work in terms of what we know rather than what we do not know. Unless the pronouncements we make are verifiable by others, they are worthless. Our job is to seek the truth. Our success depends on finding the truth and relating it to the needs and interests of man.

Some of the facts I present today will surprise many of you. I can assure you my conclusions are supported by evidence that is difficult to interpret in any other way. They may be verified by anyone who wishes to do so.

My first surprise concerns the air we breathe. Throughout my formal education I have been taught that oxygen in our atmosphere is supplied by green plants using the process of photosynthesis. It is known that plants take in carbon dioxide and, through activation by sunlight, combine it with water to make starches and cellulose and give off oxygen. In this way the whole chain of plant and animal life is sustained by energy from the sun. When the vegetable or animal materials thus produced are eaten, burned, or allowed to decay they combine with oxygen and return to the carbon dioxide and water from whence they came. We all know this. What is the surprise?

The surprise is that most of the oxygen in the atmosphere doesn't come from photosynthesis. The evidence is now overwhelming that photosynthesis is quite inadequate to have produced the amount of oxygen that is present in our atmosphere. The reason is that the amount of oxygen produced by photosynthesis is just exactly enough to convert the plant tissue back to the carbon dioxide and water from which it came. In other words, the net gain in oxygen due to photosynthesis is extremely small. The oxygen of the atmosphere had to come from another source. A most likely possibility involves the photodissociation of water vapor in the upper atmosphere by high-energy rays from the sun and by cosmic rays. This process alone could have produced, over the history of the earth . . . about seven times the present mass of oxygen in the atmosphere. Two important articles on this subject have been published in *Science* within the last eighteen months by Professors Leigh Van Valen of the University of Chicago and W. S. Broecker of Columbia University.

The significance of this information is that the supply of oxygen in the atmosphere is virtually unlimited. It is not threatened by man's activities in any significant way. If all of the organic material on earth were oxidized it would reduce the atmospheric concentration of oxygen by less than 1 percent. We can forget the depletion of oxygen of the atmosphere and get on with the solution of more serious problems.

The "Death" of Lake Erie

We have heard much in recent years about the death of Lake Erie. It is true that the beaches are no longer swimmable in the Cleveland area and that the oxygen content of the bottom of the lake is decreasing. This is called eutrophication. Heavy blame has been placed on phosphates as the cause of this situation. Housewives have been urged to curb their use of phosphate detergents. The State of New York has signed into law a measure to forbid the sale of detergents containing phosphates by 1973.

The scientific evidence I have been able to acquire on this subject shows that the cause of the eutrophication of Lake Erie has not been properly defined. This evidence suggests that if we totally stopped using phosphate detergents it would have no effect whatever on the eutrophication of Lake Erie. Many experiments have now been carried out which show that it is the organic carbon content from sewage that is using up the oxygen in the lake and not the phosphates in detergents. The reason the Cleveland area beaches are not swimmable is that the coliform bacterial count is too high, not that there is too much detergent in the water. Enlarged and improved sewage treatment facilities by Detroit, Toledo, and Cleveland will be required to correct this situation. Our garbage disposal units do far more to pollute Lake Erie than do the phosphate detergents. If we put in the proper sewage treatment facilities, the lake will sparkle blue again in a very few years.

As many of you know, the most toxic component of automobile exhaust is carbon monoxide. Each year mankind adds over 200 million tons of carbon monoxide to the atmosphere. Most of this comes from automobiles. Until this year I had been concerned about the accumulation of this toxic material because I use it daily in my research and know that it has a life in dry air of about three years. For the past several years, monitoring stations on land and sea have been measuring the carbon monoxide content of the atmosphere. Since the ratio of automobiles in the northern and southern hemispheres is 9 to 1 respectively, it was expected that the northern hemisphere would have a much higher concentration of atmospheric CO. Measurements show that there is no difference in CO amounts between the hemispheres and that the overall concentration in the air is not increasing at all.

Early in 1971, scientists at the Stanford Research Institute in Palo Alto disclosed that they had run some experiments in smog chambers containing soil. They reported that carbon monoxide rapidly disappeared from the chamber. They next sterilized the soil and found that now the carbon monoxide did not disappear. They quickly identified the organisms responsible for CO removal to be fungi of the aspergillus (bread mold) and penicillin types. These organisms, on a worldwide basis, are using all of the 200 million tons of CO made by man for their own metabolism, thus enriching the soils of the forests and the fields.

This does not say that carbon monoxide is any less toxic to man. It does say that, in spite of man's activities, this material will never build up in the atmosphere to dangerous levels except on a localized basis. To put things in perspective, let me point out that the average concentration of carbon monoxide in the Chagrin River Valley is about 1.5 parts per million. In downtown Cleveland in heavy traffic it sometimes builds up to 15 to 20 ppm. In Los Angeles it gets to be 35 ppm. In parking garages and tunnels it is sometimes 50 parts per million.

Here is another surprise for many of you. Do you know that the carbon monoxide content of cigarette smoke is 42,000 parts per million? The CO concentration in practically any smoke-filled room grossly exceeds the safety standards we permit in our laboratories. I do not mean to imply that 35 or 50 ppm of carbon monoxide should be ignored. I do mean to say that many of us subject ourselves to CO concentrations voluntarily (and involuntarily) that are greater than those of our worst polluted cities, including the Holland Tunnel in New York, without any catastrophic effects. It is not at all unusual for CO concentrations to reach the 100-200 ppm range in poorly ventilated smoke-filled rooms. If a heavy smoker spends several hours without smoking in polluted city air containing 35 ppm of CO, the concentration of CO in his blood will actually decrease! In the broad expanse of our natural air, CO levels are totally safe for human beings.

In Praise of DDT

During the past few weeks newspapers have published statements by Norman E. Borlaug, Nobel Peace Prize winner, on his opposition to the banning of DDT. [See *UNESCO Courier,* February, 1972.] Dr. Borlaug is a competent scientist. He won the Nobel prize because he was able to develop a new strain of wheat that can double the food production per acre anywhere it can be grown.

Dr. Borlaug said:

> If DDT is banned by the United States, I have wasted my life's work. I have dedicated myself to finding better methods of feeding the world's starving populations. Without DDT and other important agricultural chemicals, our goals are simply unattainable.

My investigations into this matter strongly verify the statements of Dr. Borlaug. I find that DDT has had a miraculous impact on arresting insect-borne diseases and increasing grain production from fields once ravaged by insects. According to the World Health Organization, malaria fatalities alone dropped from 4 million a year in the 1930s to less than 1 million per year in 1968. Other insect-borne diseases such as encephalitis, yellow fever and typhus fever showed similar declines. It has been estimated that 100 million human beings who would have died of these afflictions are alive today because of DDT.

DDT and other chlorinated compounds are supposedly endangering bird species by thinning of the egg shells. I am not sure this is true. The experiments I found concerning this were not conducted in such a manner that positive conclusions could be drawn from them. Even if it is true, I believe that the desirable properties of DDT so greatly outnumber the undesirable ones that it might prove to be a serious mistake to ban entirely this remarkable chemical.

Many people feel that mankind is responsible for the disappearance of animal species. I find that in some instances man may hasten the disappearance of certain species. However, the abundance of evidence indicates that he has little to do with it. About fifty species are expected to disappear during this century. But it is also true that fifty species became extinct last century and the century before that. Dr. T. H. Jukes of the University of California points out that about 100 million species of animal life have become extinct since life began on this planet about three billion years ago. Animals come and animals disappear. This is the essence of evolution as Mr. Darwin pointed out many years ago. Mankind is a relatively recent visitor here. He has had nothing to do with the disappearance of millions of species that preceded him.

Myth of the "Good Old Days"

For those who wish to return to the "good old days" when we didn't have dirty industries and automobiles to pollute the air, let's consider what life was really like in America 150 years ago. For one thing, life was very brief. The life expectancy for males was thirty-eight years. It was a grueling thirty-eight years. The work week was seventy-two hours. The average pay was $300 per year. The women's lot was even worse. They worked ninety-eight hours a week, scrubbing floors, making and washing clothes by hand, bringing in firewood, cooking in heavy iron pots and fighting off insects without screens or pesticides. Most of the clothes were rags by present-day standards. There were no fresh vegetables in winter. Vitamin-deficiency diseases were prevalent. Homes were cold in winter and sweltering in summer.

Every year an epidemic could be expected and chances were high that it would carry off someone in your family. If you think that water pollution is bad now, it was more deadly then. In 1793, one person in every five in the city of Philadelphia died in a single epidemic of typhoid fever as a result of polluted water. Many people of that time never heard a symphony orchestra or traveled more than twenty miles from their birthplace during their entire lives. . . . I wonder how many informed people want to return to the "paradise" of 150 years ago. Perhaps the simple life is not so simple.

Many of us are alarmed by the dire announcements from technically untrained people and from scientists who have not bothered to check their assumptions against the evidence. We have gone off half-cocked with expensive measures in some cases to solve problems that are more imaginary than real. For example . . . [in March 1971], Governor [John] Gilligan [of Ohio] "declared war on pollution in general, on thermal pollution in particular and specifically on the controversial Davis-Bresse nuclear power plant being built."

Investigation of the thermal-pollution problem reveals that, beyond any question of doubt, the sun is by far the greatest thermal polluter of Lake Erie. Governor Gilligan announced that he would "back legislation making it unlawful to increase the temperature of the (effluent) water by more than one degree over the natural temperature." As we all know, the natural temperature of the lake is changed by the sun more than 40°F every year between winter (33°) and summer (75 + °). The natural life in the lake accommodates this drastic change in great fashion, as it has for many thousands of years.

I have determined that if we could store up all of the electricity produced in Ohio in a whole year and use it exclusively for heating Lake Erie all at one time, it would heat the entire lake less than three tenths of one degree (0.3°F).

In terms of localized heating, we must remember that we already have many hundreds of power plants pouring warm water into streams and lakes. Twenty-two of these are nuclear power plants. Evaluation of the effect of these from an ecological point of view is that "thermal pollution" is a less descriptive and less appropriate term than is "thermal enrichment." There are no species disappearing. No ecological catastrophes or problems have appeared. Some of the best fishing locations in the country are near the warm water outlets of power plants.

In every age we have people practicing witchcraft in one form or another. I used to think that the people of New England were particularly irrational in accusing certain women of being witches without evidence to prove it. Suppose someone accused you of being a witch. How could you prove you were not? It is impossible to prove negative evidence. Yet precisely this same witchcraft practice is being used to deter the construction of nuclear power plants. The opponents are saying that these plants are witches and it is up to the builders to prove that they are not.

The scientific evidence is that the nuclear power plants, constructed to this date, are the cleanest and least polluting devices for generating electricity so far developed by man. We need the electricity to maintain the standard of living we have reached.

From what we read and hear it would seem that we are on the edge of impending doom. A scientific evaluation of the evidence does not support this conclusion. We clearly have some undesirable problems attributed to technological activities. The solution of these problems will require a technical understanding of their nature. The problems cannot be solved unless they are properly identified. This will require more technically trained people not less. These problems cannot be solved by legislation unless the legislators understand the technical nature of the problem. In my estimation, the most serious problem we face is the rapidly increasing human population on a worldwide basis. The pollution of our natural waters with sewage and chemicals is perhaps the second most serious one. Nothing good has been found for either sulfur oxides or particulate matter in our air. Hydrocarbon emissions from our automobiles can be hazardous, especially in poorly ventilated locations. I have not been able to identify any problems that we do not already know how to solve. It is strictly a question of economics. The back-to-nature approach of withdrawing from reality will accomplish nothing.

Get the Facts

I believe, as Thomas Jefferson did, that if the public is properly informed, the people will make wise decisions. I know that the public has not been getting all of the scientific facts on many matters relating to ecology. That is why I am speaking out on this subject today as a scientist and as a citizen. Some of the things you have heard may be contrary to your beliefs but I am willing to support my conclusions on evidence good enough for me to stake my reputation on it.

In summary let me remind you that my studies suggest that we are not on the brink of disaster. The world's oxygen supply is secure. There will be no buildup of poisonous carbon monoxide. Our waters can be made pure again by adequate treatment plants. The disappearance of species is natural. We cannot solve our real problems unless we attack them on the basis of what we know rather than what we don't know. We must use our knowledge and not our fears to solve the real problems of our environment.

We are all familiar with the Aesop fable about the shepherd boy and the wolf. He tended his master's sheep near a dark forest not far from the village. He found sheepwatching to be somewhat dull and unamusing.

His master had told him to call for help should a wolf attack the flock, and the villagers would come to the rescue. Although he had not seen anything that even looked like a wolf, he ran toward the village shouting at the top of his voice, "Wolf! Wolf!"

As he expected, the villagers who heard the cry dropped their work and ran in great excitement to the pasture. But when they got there they found that the boy had put in a false alarm for his own amusement.

A few days later the shepherd boy again shouted, "Wolf! Wolf!" Once more the villagers ran to help him, only to be laughed at again.

Then one evening as the sun was setting behind the forest and the shadows were creeping out over the pasture, a wolf really did spring from the underbrush and fall upon the sheep.

In terror, the boy ran toward the village shouting, "Wolf! Wolf!" Although the villagers heard his cry, they did not run to help him as they had before. "He cannot fool us again," they said.

The results were disastrous for the boy and his sheep.

The moral is, Those who are found to misrepresent facts are not believed even when they speak the truth.

In recent months, we have heard cries of wolf with respect to our oxygen supply, the buildup of carbon monoxide, the disappearance of species, DDT, phosphates in the lake, thermal pollution, radiation effects on health from nuclear power plants, the Amchitka nuclear tests, lead in gasoline, and mercury in fish, to name a few. For the most part, these cries have not been malicious but have been based largely on fear, ignorance or misinformation. The people have listened to these cries and have come running to the rescue but they are not finding many wolves.

Let us not cry wolf until we are reasonably certain that we have done enough homework to know what a wolf looks like. Otherwise we may undermine our credibility and not be believed by the people when we warn them of the real wolves that do exist.

KEEPING THE MOVEMENT IN PERSPECTIVE [4]

The environmental pessimism of today has its roots in the writings of Thomas Malthus. Reflecting on the misery of eighteenth century man, . . . Malthus postulated a "constant tendency for all animated life to increase beyond the nourishment prepared for it." Malthus reasoned that a geometric rate of increase would, unless checked, outstrip the

[4] From "A Critical Appraisal of the Environmental Movement," by Ron S. Boster, an expert in hydrology and water resources and an economist with the United States Forest Service. *Journal of Forestry*. 69:12-16. Ja. '71. Reprinted by permission.

food supply, which increased arithmetically. "Except for
Marx's prediction of progressive pauperization of workers
under capitalism, Malthus' was probably the worst forecast
ever made by an economist" [writes economist Henry C.
Wallich].

The essential ingredient in the classical economists'
theory was that natural resources are inherently *limited or
fixed,* thereby limiting potential human welfare. Mankind
was doomed, and could look forward only to a subsistence
level of existence.

The technological revolution preceded, then overlapped,
the conservation movement in this country. The technical
revolution enabled men to get more output for a given energy
input, or conversely, the same output for less energy. Man
was being freed from his age-old tie to the land and to agriculture as the basic cornerstone of his economy.

The conservation movement of seventy years ago was a
direct outgrowth of Malthusian thought. The conservationists were convinced that the private sector was short-chang-
ing future generations by accelerating the exploitation of
natural resources. They were disillusioned with laissez faire
capitalism as it pertained to natural resources and saw land
resources as limited. The "cowboy economy" whereby people
exploit, and then push on to greener pastures, was coming
to an end. By accepting the scarcity doctrine, the conservationists were actually trying to *forestall* an impending
disaster.

With the benefit of hindsight, it may be argued that
conservationists were doing the right things, but for the
wrong reasons. The "in" thing to believe today is that
Malthus was right. But the fact is that only *at a given point
in time and space* is the supply of natural resources fixed
because man's knowledge and therefore, his technology, are
also fixed only at one point in time and space. In economic
parlance, the supply of natural resources is perfectly inelastic
in the short run. However, over time we observe that man
learns new ways to exploit his environment, the supply of

natural resources becomes elastic over the long run, and, therefore, the supply of natural resources *increases*.

This may be difficult to digest in view of the physical confines of the "spaceship earth." But living in a closed system affects human welfare, not merely by limiting resources, but also by posing threats to health and happiness in the form of a deteriorating environment.

Natural resources must be defined in terms of man and man's knowledge. This is not a matter of mere semantics; it is absurd to define resources otherwise. To quote Barnet and Morse in their classic study, *Scarcity and Growth: The Economics of Natural Resource Availability*:

> Recognition of the possibility of technical progress clearly cuts the ground from under the concept of Malthusian scarcity. Resources can only be defined in terms of known technology. Half a century ago the air was for breathing and burning; now it is also a natural resource of the chemical industry. Two decades ago Vermont granite was only building and tombstone material; now it is a potential fuel, each ton of which has a usable energy content (uranium) equal to fifty tons of coal. The notion of an absolute limit to natural resources availability is untenable when the definition of resources changes drastically and unpredictably over time.

The tremendous economic growth in some countries following the industrial-technological revolution raises the question of why some countries have prospered while others, sometimes endowed with a greater supply of natural resources, have not. The technological revolution has enabled development of ubiquitous (extensive) resources as substitutes for scarce (intensive) resources. Japan, endowed with little in the form of physical resources and with a high population density, is able to prosper. Great Britain, on a par with Japan in terms of resources, and having a lower population density, is waning economically due to social institutions that impede economic prosperity. Many countries richly endowed with natural resources have made very little progress.

A stock supply of natural resources is less important in providing increased human welfare than the social, economic, political, and moral institutions of society. The environmental movement would do well to cleanse itself of the notion of physical resource scarcity. Short-run instances of actual resource scarcity have occurred in the past and will undoubtedly occur in the future. Such shortages have, however, generally been very small, short-lived, and highly localized. Concern over "running out of resources" should be put to more constructive uses, such as preserving resource amenities, preventing further environmental deterioration, reducing pollution levels, and preserving irreplaceable and unique resources for future generations.

Internal Conflicts

The environmental movement is split into several causes: population, water pollution, air pollution, and wilderness, to name only a few. This split poses a problem because it is not always a complementary or supplementary relationship that exists between two or more uses of the same natural resource. People join the environmental movement for many reasons; they bring with them personal wants and a personal ordering of values. The result is that even within divisions of the movement, there are significant differences of opinion as to what goals and means should be.

The wants and desires of private individuals and private groups are not always retained in public groups. When individuals come together they bring different mixes of wants and desires, and the combination of these are translated into policies and programs that may differ substantially from the preference rankings of the individuals within the group. In defense of environmentalists, however, it seems that their planning horizons are often longer than the planning horizons of public groups. There often appears to be more concern for the future by environmentalists than by government.

Additional conflicts that hamper the effectiveness of the environmental movement arise between different public institutions (i.e., Federal versus state, state versus local interests) and between present and future wants resulting from different time-planning horizons, different discounting rates, and different marginal utilities by different persons and groups of persons. There are also important conflicts over the *use* of land resources: should this area be a wilderness, or developed for multiple-use recreation; should this canyon be left in its pristine state or should a multipurpose concrete monolith be built? Disputes over urban zoning bring the same conflicts to the fore.

The environmental crisis is hardly a result of technological inability to solve the problems. Most of us would agree that tremendous steps could be taken with current technology. The overriding constraints are social institutions, interpersonal relations, individual wants, desires, values, and human nature.

There are many who are opposed to what the environmentalists are advocating, even some of the environmentalists themselves. There can be no criteria for solving the problems that would be agreeable to all. It is not only a question of us "bird-and-bunny" protagonists against the industrial and technological giants; conflicts *within* the environmental movement pose serious obstacles to the development of a more livable environment.

Is Survival at Stake?

Is the environmental crisis a question of survival? Despite the yellow press articles, there are few who have gone or will go so far as to claim that mankind faces extinction if the environment is not cleaned up. The threat of nuclear war or nuclear accident surely poses more of a threat to survival than environmental pollution.

This is not to minimize the ecological problems: the frightening buildups of pesticide residues, the plight of endangered species, and, in general, the man-caused grief imposed on other living things. We do not know what price will be paid by future generations for our extravagance. Should we allow environmental deterioration to continue, man's fate may be worse than extinction.

A large portion of the air pollution controversy is over aesthetics—questions of human values. This is not to deny that air pollution is a serious health problem, but to point out that aesthetics play an *important* role in air pollution in addition to valid health concerns.

A case has been made for a strong association between morbidity and mortality and air pollution, and a relationship between air pollution and respiratory diseases of all kinds has been documented. With regard to water pollution, however, only in rare instances has it threatened the public health. But our unwillingness to stop the increase in water pollution results in more and more cases of water pollution health problems. Health is a very real component of the environmental crisis, but only one *part* of the environmental crisis.

For the developed countries, the environmental crisis is not a population problem based on too few resources. The American populationists are led by Paul Ehrlich, a noted population biologist, but a naive Malthusian resource economist. The philosophy behind this movement is that there is a finite stock of resources and that because the United States accounts for nearly one half of the planet's annual resource consumption, the United States is hastening disaster.

Disasters such as starvation and famine will occur, and are occurring now, but not because the rich countries have depleted the *stock* of natural resources and deprived the overpopulated countries of their just due. Disasters would not be averted by the rich countries reducing their resource gluttony. To paraphrase Wallich: If my friend is dangerously overweight and I tell him to diet, does that mean that I, too, should diet, even though I am fit and trim?

The full consequences of a national population policy ought to be considered. The total number of people is only one parameter of the population. To ignore other parameters, such as average, mode, and median ages, and the skewness of the age distribution may result in undesirable age distributions. A desirable age distribution is as important as, and possibly more important than, the total number of people. In this regard, the populationists have been guilty of tunnel vision. The reasoning of the populationists could have consequences for foreign relations. The total effect is to make starving peoples believe that the United States and other wealthy nations are responsible for their hunger.

It is also possible that science, as a meaningful endeavor of man, will suffer from the impact of these theories because many scientists are stepping outside their areas of competency, venturing into areas remote to their fields, and making judgments that may lead to a mistrust of science.

Population and Pollution

Many populationists believe, and would have us believe, that pollution is the result of increased population. This is only partly true. People-pollution at Yellowstone is not so much the result of population increases as of increased affluence; air pollution is not just the result of more people, but also of people owning more and bigger cars than in the past. It is not just consumption of resources that contributes to pollution but perhaps more importantly, per capita consumption. There seems little reason why cutting the growth of the population would have any effect other than to increase the per capita consumption of resources over time. Hence, I believe the argument can be made that a stabilized population would not necessarily decrease pollution. I agree with René Dubos who states:

> Environmental degradation and loss in the quality of life will continue to accelerate very rapidly in the United States even if we succeed in achieving zero population growth. The impact of technology therefore constitutes a more immediate threat than the population bomb and far more destructive because many of its effects will be irreversible.

Few minority persons are active in the environmental movement, which is essentially composed of upper-class and upper-middle-class persons—defined in terms of attitudes if not income. Less affluent persons outside the movement must

gain small comfort by constantly being told it is they who
stand to benefit the most from an improved environment.

A ghetto *is* a terrible place in which to live, but it does
not follow that cleaner air, fewer freeways, more wilderness
areas, more national parks, and more forest recreation areas
will improve the welfare of the ghetto resident. Like all of
us, the poor will have to pay. Not everybody will pay equally;
nor will everyone benefit equally. The cost of environmental
improvements to the poor must be considered. Before we can
say it is to the poor's advantage to join the club, we should
tell them what the dues are going to be.

Populationists believe that it is the rich not the poor,
who are hastening environmental deterioration and a decline in social welfare. They argue that because the rich are
more resource-intensive, affluent additions to the population
are of more consequence than poor additions. It is difficult
to believe that social welfare, and certainly the welfare of
the poor, can be increased by placing the emphasis of population reduction on the rich rather than the poor. Such a
policy would likely make the rich richer, and the poor poorer.
It is a "Robin Hood upside-down policy."

What Are We Fighting For?

I have argued that the environmental movement is based
on faulty Malthusian reasoning and that it is fragmented
into camps which may not be able to reach mutually agreeable solutions. I have also argued that the environmental
crisis is not a question of resource scarcity and that the population bomb and potential human extinction are overrated.
The crisis is rightfully related to public health concerns, but
this is not all-inclusive. Environmentalists have tended to
be selfish by imposing their values on others and have been
lax in viewing the distributional cost impact of providing a
higher quality environment. What, then, is the saving grace
of the environmental movement?

[Professor John V.] Krutilla argues that the "central issue
is providing for the present and future the amenities *asso-*

ciated with unspoiled natural environments, for which the market fails to make adequate provisions." With this view, traditional notions of conservation economics—"the optimal intertemporal utilization of fixed resource stocks" are open to question.

[Warren C.] Robinson [a land economist] has noted that virgin areas are not an absolute requirement for life, health, or productivity, that only in exceptional cases does one encounter an area that is irreproducible, and that amenities are not collective consumption items, which is to say that left to its own devices, the private market *would* provide these, i.e., the market may not have broken down as most would assume. Certainly virgin areas are not necessary, but, in the short run, neither are virgins. Yet I would argue that both are highly desirable in a viable society. To argue that the market has not broken down in providing resource amenities is a question of degree; the same argument could be made regarding other public-provided goods such as bridges or highways.

No one argues that the Grand Canyon is replaceable, yet there is some debate as to its potential for multiple use. Other areas, not as well-known, are the current battlegrounds. Whether or not these areas are reproducible depends upon whose side you are on at a given point in time.

Robinson raises another question of interest: "We are all inured by now to planner's preferences riding roughshod over market preferences from time to time even in capitalist societies. But would we really be comfortable about Government supplying amenities if Government also had to spend money educating people to enjoy them?" If others, including Government agencies, must make normative judgments as to the propriety of environmental activities, then there is room for criticism. Again, we are caught up in a problem of values and value judgments.

The environmental movement fight is over amenities— saving what we have, enhancing what we have, *creating* what we can. Contrary to the beliefs of many, amenities *can* be created. While it is true that, once destroyed, many amenities are lost forever, it does not follow that the supply is fixed. A park can be created from a garbage dump; a forest can be grown where strip mining once soured the landscape. Who would deny that such renovated areas are not producers of resource amenities? The fight should not be confined to wilderness or bucolic areas, because the crisis exists as well in urban and suburban areas. The environmentalists' failure to deal with the working environment of urban workers was commented upon by [former Secretary of the Interior] Stuart Udall:

> In short, the blue-collar worker suffers from an environmental neglect that is overwhelming. Environmental groups, above all act as if the blue-collar workers did not exist. Their lack of concern for his workplace—their failure even in recognizing it as an environment—is the most glaring defect in their young movement.

Conservation is just as relevant, perhaps more so, in densely inhabited areas where most of us work and spend our leisure time. We must realize that amenities are value-related, just as environmental quality is value-related.

The Solutions

We have three general alternatives:
1. Continue with present trends.
2. Modify present trends.
3. Go back to nature.

The first alternative is not a solution, and the last is acceptable only to a few environmental radicals. The answer lies with the second alternative.

We must first develop new indicators of economic growth and human welfare and evolve away from the gross national product as the prime index of the health and welfare of this and other countries. We need acceptable new indices of quality.

"Now or never" political pronouncements are useful in generating public concern which in turn may lead to constructive progress. Recently announced Government agency reshuffling may have some positive effect. Far more important, however, is the need to *adopt specific goals and set deadlines.*

The foregoing requirements are necessary, but not sufficient. A change in political atmosphere from pessimism to optimism, is also crucial. A genuine atmosphere of optimism and dedication is necessary to insure against acceptance of failure. What was true for the moon program is true for the environmental crisis. Real progress can only be made when we share the desire and the will to spend the necessary funds and make the necessary sacrifices for environmental improvement and preservation. This can only come about under an umbrella of dedicated optimism, and this atmosphere must emanate from the highest offices of public trust.

We are faced with a complex and dynamic system wherein technology interacts with, and is constrained by, social institutions. The real environmental crisis is institutional, not technological; it is a question of culture more than a question of resources. The problem must be conceptualized in this framework, and the solution must be viewed as minimization, not elimination, of pollution in view of institutional and technological constraints. Certainly, the institutional constraints are of far more consequence to the environmental crisis than technological constraints. Because the problem is dynamic and related strongly to human values, the solutions will be dynamic and related to human values.

The problem is how to provide an arena wherein values can be expressed and register their influence to effect the required institutional changes. Our system of government is far from perfect, and is in need of changes, but it is the best system of government for solving these problems. [As Adlai Stevenson once put it:] We travel together, passengers on a little spaceship, dependent on its vulnerable supplies of air and soil . . . , preserved from annihilation only by the care, the work, and I say the love, we give our fragile craft.

III. THE DEBATE ON GROWTH

EDITOR'S INTRODUCTION

Recently a team of experts from the Massachusetts Institute of Technology set out to determine, on a systematic and scientific basis, whether there are any worldwide limits to economic growth. Using present trends in world population, industrialization, pollution, food production, and resource depletion as their basic tools of measurement, they concluded that even under the most optimistic circumstances —including major technological breakthroughs—the limits to growth would be reached by the year 2100, or less than 130 years from now. If circumstances so conspired, the limits could come even sooner—within the lifetime of some children alive today. "The most probable result [of reaching the limits]," the report concluded, "will be a rather sudden and uncontrollable decline in both population and industrial capacity." The prospect is, in short, that unless the trends are halted our grandchildren or great-grandchildren will live to witness the greatest crisis ever to befall mankind.

The MIT study stirred as much attention and controversy as Britain's "Blueprint for Survival." (See "Muddling Our Way to Extinction," in Section I, above.) But it also served to focus worldwide attention on what is rapidly becoming the crux of the entire survival-or-annihilation debate: the extent to which our planet's limited resources can afford further economic growth or progress. That subject is the main concern of this section.

In the first, introductory, article, the editors of the Foreign Policy Association give a balanced account of the controversy to date. The conclusions reached thus far present far more questions than answers. The second article is a straightforward tract by journalists Wade Greene and Soma Golden on behalf of the views of British economist Ezra J. Mishan, once derided but now taken seriously. Mishan is described as the world's foremost apostle of doubt about the blessings of economic and technological growth. The somewhat cranky quality of his personality, as the authors point out, should not deflect us from the cogency of his arguments. In the last article, a correspondent for the New York *Times* sets forth in considered words the practical implications of the debate for an economy such as that of the United States.

THE LIMITS TO GROWTH [1]

"If the present growth trends in world population, industrialization, pollution, food production, and resources depletion continue unchanged, the limits to growth on this planet will be reached sometime within the next one hundred years." This is the thesis of *The Limits to Growth,* a controversial study by an MIT team led by Dennis Meadows. It was commissioned and financed by the Club of Rome, an international group of environmentally concerned technocrats and businessmen as part of the club's Project on the Predicament of Mankind.

Using a model developed by computer expert Professor Jay Forrester of MIT, the Meadows team translated five growth trends and their interlocking relationships into mathematical terms. They found that even under the most optimistic circumstances—including unanticipated technological breakthroughs of major significance, the limits to

[1] From *Great Decisions 1973.* Fact Sheet No. 6: "Man on Earth: Can He Control His Environment?" Foreign Policy Association. 345 E. 46th St. New York 10017. '73. p 65-6. Reprinted with permission from *Great Decisions 1973.* Copyright 1973 by The Foreign Policy Association, Inc.

growth would be reached by the year 2100 if present trends
continue.

The most probable result will be a rather sudden and uncontrollable decline in both population and industrial capacity.

Population cannot grow without food [they reason]; food
production is increased by growth of capital [more tractors, fertilizers, pesticides]; more capital requires more resources; discarded
resources become pollution; pollution interferes with the growth
of both population and food.

The key to *The Limits of Growth* findings is the assump-
tion that the five major growth trends—population, industrialization, food production, depletion of resources and environmental degradation—increase by geometric progression
(1, 2, 4, 8, 16, etc.) rather than by adding increments (1, 2,
3, 4, 5, etc.). Growth thus is slow at the beginning but in a
short time reaches a staggering level. To illustrate the point,
the authors cite the Persian legend of the clever courtier who
presented a chessboard to the king and asked the king to
give him in return one grain of rice for the first square on
the board, two grains for the second, four grains for the
third, eight grains for the fourth, and so on. By the fortieth
square one million million grains of rice had to be brought
from the royal granary. Long before the last square was
reached, the storehouse was empty.

Collapse can only be avoided, according to the authors,
if we are prepared to limit growth and settle for a condition
of economic and ecological stability. Population should be
stabilized by equalizing birth and death rates. Industrial
growth must stop except to replace old facilities. Behavioral
patterns must change: we must learn to prefer services, such
as education and recreation, to material goods.

How valid are these findings? Must we abandon what
has become an article of faith common to East and West,
industrialized and developing nations alike, namely growth?

Narrow Limits

The mathematical formulas used in *The Limits of
Growth,* some critics assert, oversimplify reality, and there-

fore the conclusions based on them are faulty. Little allow-
ance is made, for example, for the human factor—for man's
problem-solving capabilities and his capacity to alter and
adapt his behavior.

Many of the MIT team's assumptions are at best questionable, other critics charge. *The Limits of Growth,* according to the review in the New York *Times Book Review,* "is
best summarized not as a rediscovery of the laws of nature
but as a rediscovery of the oldest maxim of computer science:
Garbage In, Garbage Out." Chided *The Economist,* a British
newsweekly: in 1872 any scientist could have proved, by pro-
jecting current trends, that by the 1970s urban transport
and travel within London would be impossible (and therefore a city the size of London was impossible) "because
where were Londoners going to stable all the horses and how
could they avoid being asphyxiated by the manure?"

The "risk of collapse" is built into the model, other critics
contend: while the authors assume that the five trends grow
geometrically, they also assume that other factors which
could offset the trends, such as new technology and the dis-
covery of new resources or man-made substitutes, grow at a
far slower rate.

Technological innovations, many maintain, hold infinite
promise for the future. Foolproof contraceptive methods,
the production of protein from fossil fuels, the generation
or harnessing of virtually limitless energy, including pollu-
tion-free solar energy—these are some of the discoveries that
could make the MIT team's projections meaningless. We
have already seen pollution controls work, notably in London, where the average hours of winter sunlight nearly
doubled in fifteen years (at a cost of 36 cents per person a
year to clean the air). More than forty kinds of fish now
thrive along one section of the Thames where none existed
only ten years ago.

The authors assume that industrial and agricultural
growth use up resources and generate pollution. But, some

critics note, it is possible to conceive of certain forms of industrial growth, say increases in computer capacity, which could result in dramatic increases in economic growth with only negligible pollution or resources drain.

As to natural resources, critics charge that the authors do not adequately take into account the "economic fact" that as resources become scarce, their price goes up and either substitutes are found or man learns to do without.

Finally, the authors are criticized both for solving complex problems by the simple expedient of assuming a halt in all sources of change and for claiming that their solution is something new. A century or two ago, critics recall, Malthus and John Stuart Mill also claimed that the only hope for survival was a "stationary state," to be achieved by limiting population and wealth.

The Options

Meadows is the first to admit that the model is not perfect, but the world, he insists, cannot wait for perfect models and total understanding. He insists that "we don't have any alternative [to limiting growth]. It's not as though we can choose to keep growing or not. We are certainly going to stop growing. The question is, do we do it in a way that is most consistent with our goals or do we just let nature take its course."

Among those who have analyzed Meadows' findings, many are convinced that there are alternatives. [World Bank President Robert] McNamara, for one, takes an optimistic view of the future.

As the affluent nations continue to take their environmental problems more seriously, they are going to discover a whole new range of technology to abate and avoid ecological dangers. The less-privileged countries can adapt these technical advances to their own local conditions.

Meadows disagrees: technology is the problem, not the solution. Technological optimism, Meadows contends, is "the most common and the most dangerous reaction to our findings." Technology can relieve symptoms of a problem without affecting underlying causes. "To pretend that growth can go on forever," comments the New York *Times'* Anthony Lewis, "is like arguing that the earth is flat. Only the consequences are more serious."

"Selective growth," others suggest, is preferable to a total freeze. If all growth is frozen, we would have to write off the possibility of cleaning up the environment, whereas if growth is selective it could lead eventually to even less waste and pollution than the "equilibrium state."

What is needed, according to sociologist Frank Reissman, is a "shift in growth from the traditional industrial area to the human-service, or people-serving sphere." We should abandon the old yardstick, which measures progress in terms of the accumulation of material goods, and substitute a yardstick which measures improvements in the quality of life. Instead of striving for a larger gross national product (GNP), we should aim instead at raising the "gross national utility," to borrow a phrase from Sicco L. Mansholt, president of the Commission of the European Communities. We must, in short, adopt a new ethic and new values.

The debate over growth has only begun, but already major issues are emerging. Is it true that growth must end sooner or later on this finite planet? Is it possible to move from growth to a state of equilibrium? Is it desirable? And if it is, do we have the political will to initiate and accept the tough decisions required to achieve equilibrium? Are the poor countries to be frozen at or near subsistence levels? Must the world's resources be equitably divided? If so, how? If survival is at stake, can decisions be left in private hands? If not, is world government the answer?

For the present, there are more immediate questions that beg answers. The nations that met in Stockholm [see Section V below] are committed to improving the environment. Who will pay the bill and how will responsibility be apportioned? Are new institutions needed to cope with the problems of the environment?

THE CURSE OF THE GNP [2]

"You could very comfortably have stopped growing after the First World War," said the bearded Englishman the other day, in a clipped Manchester accent, over a cup of tea. "There was enough technology to make life quite pleasant. Cities weren't overgrown. People weren't too avaricious. You hadn't really ruined the environment as you have now, and built up entrenched industries so you can't go back."

Oh? Did he mean that in a half-century in which average per capita income in the United States has more than quintupled and technology has created whole new modes of transportation, communication, medicine and agriculture, there has been no notable improvement in our country's or our countrymen's lot? He does indeed, it becomes disconsolately clear; Ezra J. Mishan is perhaps the world's foremost apostle of doubt about the blessings of economic and technological growth.

The "Mishanic message," as some of his academic colleagues have sardonically dubbed it, is embodied in three books, a dozen articles and countless lectures. It is part economics, part social philosophy and no small measure of personal moralizing. It ranges from the coolly academic to the acerbically witty, from the direly prophetic to the downright crotchety. And it has attracted a broad, ideologically diverse following. At least parts of it have, that is; it is doubtful that anyone but Ezra Mishan would subscribe to it all. The heart of the message is the singularly un-American, if no longer uncommon, heresy that economic growth and its underlying spur, technological innovation, are not necessarily good things, and that certain types of growth are proving to be wretchedly bad for affluent societies. In possibly the most succinct capsulization of his wordsome gospel, Mishan declared recently: "I am not one of those who believe that the original Luddites were wholly wrong."

[2] From "The Luddites Were Not All Wrong," by Wade Greene, a specialist on social and environmental problems, and Soma Golden, Washington correspondent for *Business Week*. New York *Times Magazine*. p 40-2+. N. 21, '71. © 1971 by The New York Times Company. Reprinted by permission.

The swelling ranks of the environment-minded have been voicing skepticism of late about specific sorts of economic and technological development, but the Mishanic message not only has a broader sweep, it also bears a special authority. For it issues in effect from the high priesthood of growth itself. Mishan is an economist, a reader at the London School of Economics; for the last two years he taught as well at American University in Washington, D.C., and he just finished a series of lectures at Johns Hopkins. As an economist, he is a member of a breed of social scientist who, since World War II, have preached economic growth as a principal article of faith. "Among the faithful," writes Mishan, "and they are legion, any doubt that, say, a 4-percent growth rate is better for the nation than a 3-percent growth rate . . . is tantamount to a doubt that 4 is greater than 3."

As advisers to presidents and premiers, the faithful, moreover, have powerfully practiced as well as preached their faith, directing fiscal and monetary policy onward and, above all, upward, toward the perpetual vision of a grosser Gross National Product. Just such a vision was held forth in fact as an ultimate blessing of and justification for President Nixon's new economic program [announced August 15, 1971]. Paul W. McCracken, [former] chairman of the President's Council of Economic Advisers, contentedly predicted that the program would add $15 billion to the GNP.

The Perils of Growthmanship

Heresy is none too strong a term for Mishan's challenge to the faith—not in an increasingly secular and materialistic civilization that regards economic growth as virtually identical with human advancement. Mishan's gospel of doubt would be notable enough in itself therefore, but Mishan, it appears, is by no means a lonely heretic in the priesthood of growth. Though he was one of the earliest and is one of the most articulate of economists to question growth, there is something of a crisis of confidence brewing throughout the economic profession these days concerning the ultimate beneficence of growth and the ultimate significance of the Gross National Product as a barometer of social virtue and vitality.

The so-called father of the GNP, Harvard professor emeritus Simon S. Kuznets, who last month [October 1971] was awarded the Nobel prize in economics for his studies of economic growth, has long insisted on the limitations of the GNP as a guide for long-term economic policy. And the profession that turned his national income measurements into the GNP three decades ago—and at least acquiesced in its use as just such a guide—is now beginning to agree about the limitations of the GNP, having watched this economic measurement soar accompanied by even faster-climbing indexes of crime, pollution and congestion.

Some of the country's most prestigious economic research organizations such as the National Bureau of Economic Research and Resources for the Future, Inc., and even the Federal Government's Office of Management and the Budget, are looking for new ways to measure the attainments of American life, and a number of economists in these groups and elsewhere are willing to at least entertain the possibility that on some more encompassing social scale than the GNP, we aren't doing very well at all.

Mishan has no doubts about his own doubts in this regard and has, in fact, coined a small lexicon of negative words to convey his negative thoughts about the drift of expanding Western economics. We are producing many "bads" as well as goods, he feels, contributing to people's "illfare" or "diswelfare" as well as their welfare, often "uglifying" instead of beautifying, increasing the "disamenities" of life and creating sprawling "subtopias," realms that are decidedly this side of paradise. Mishan has also established a technological demonology, in which the baddest demon is indisputably the automobile.

I once wrote that the invention of the automobile was one of the greatest disasters to have befallen mankind [Mishan recently told an audience at Vassar]. I have had time since to reflect on this statement and to revise my judgment to the effect that the automobile is *the* greatest disaster to have befallen mankind. . . .

For sheer irresistible destructive power, nothing—except perhaps the airliner—can compare with it. Almost every principle of architectural harmony has been perverted in the vain struggle to keep the mounting volume of motorized traffic moving through our cities, towns, resorts, hamlets and, of course, through our rapidly expanding suburbs. Clamor, dust, fumes, congestion and visual distraction are the predominant features in all built-up areas. . . . Whether we are in Paris, Chicago, Tokyo, Düsseldorf or Milan, it is the choking din and the endless movement of motorized traffic that dominates the scene. As well we might try to enjoy the variety of a six-course banquet while suffering from a throbbing toothache. . . .

If Mishan had his way, the private automobile would be banned from the face of the earth.

There is a good deal of other paraphernalia that Mishan feels we could and should do without, too. He sheds his economist's cloak of neutrality about goods and services to brand much of the outpouring of Western economies, and particularly that of the United States, as trivial at best—the mass-produced "near-rubbish" of a "throw-away society," he says.

The impression of a casual observer in the United States watching an endless stream of twenty-ton trucks hurtling through the night, from East to West and from West to East, is that here, indeed, are the visible manifestations of economic power and prosperity [he writes in a recent issue of *Encounter* magazine]. The freight, however, ranges from dish-washing machines to electronic bugging devices, from electric toothbrushes to plastic baubles and from cosmetics to frozen television suppers. Much that serves [only] to gratify the thoughtless whims of people slouched disconsolately before a television screen serves also as the foundation of vast industries whose outputs form a sizable proportion of the nation's annual product.

A leading academic acquaintance refers to Mishan as a "reformed Victorian." And one detects a high quotient of plain fuddyduddiness in the fifty-three-year-old economist's jaundiced view of contemporary life. In *Costs of Economic*

Growth—Mishan's first lay-oriented book on his central theme—he laments the loss of an "essential sweetness" in the passing of "once-common domestic occasions" such as listening to one's daughter playing the piano or harpsichord. Thanks, he grumbles, to the incursion of the record player. He tends to take a stern Victorian stance on changing sexual mores. He told us he deplored younger people's "defiance against every known taboo in society and their attempt to break through in some way or another and achieve happiness through pathological excesses." He sees greed and avarice at work everywhere and with Biblical righteousness that sounds a good deal closer to Elmer Gantry than, say, Paul Samuelson, he frequently scores the weakness and venality of men. Indeed, there seems to be little about contemporary life that pleases or reassures him.

The Power of Negative Thinking

Mishan confesses that when he showed a draft of his first book to a student at the London School of Economics, the young man advised him to scrap the thing—because it sounded "too much like my father." It would be easy, in fact, to dismiss Mishan's arguments as simply the complaints of upper middle age against a rapidly changing world. But economists and other careful readers of Mishan are not inclined to do so readily. This is because underneath his occasionally cranky preachments is a hard core of economic reasoning. "Mishan is an original," remarks Milton Friedman, the prominent University of Chicago economist who was Mishan's adviser when the Englishman took his doctor's degree at Chicago. But Friedman quickly adds, "I have great respect for his analytical competence." In fact, Mishan has an enviable academic reputation built on years of orthodox work in his special field of welfare economics. This is a highly analytical, mathematical and theoretical branch of economics dealing with the effects of economic activity on social welfare. The sort of thing that Mishan has grappled with is determining what type of tax structure—income, excise or otherwise—is ideal in terms of optimum distribution of a society's goods and services. Mishan's rigorous and ornately geometric papers are considered to be among the major work being done in welfare economics. Mishan is also a leading academic expert in the related field of cost-benefit analysis, and has just had a book published in this highly technical area.

It is from such solid underpinnings that Mishan launches his scornful critiques. And despite his many arguments with traditional economics he frames his own antigrowth gospels in strictly traditional economic terms. Central to Mishan's questioning of economic growth, of the postwar variety at least, is the venerable economic idea of "external diseconomies" or "spillovers"—side-effects of economic activity that don't enter into the prices that people buy or sell things for. A classic example of a spillover is the damage done downwind from a smokestack, to painted surfaces, clothes, lungs. British Lord Alfred Marshall introduced the idea in the early 1900s, and ever since, economists have set aside a few paragraphs on spillovers in general textbooks. But because it is hard and sometimes impossible to put a price tag on spillover effects, economists have been reluctant to deal with them.

Besides, spillovers once did not seem very important in the broader economic scheme of things. Air pollution and water pollution, two of the major spillovers of industrial production, were in fact pretty small matters in less crowded and industrialized times. But as Mishan and a growing number of economists now see it, such "bads" of modern production (and sometimes consumption; e.g., the exhausts of millions of autos) are becoming a very sizable matter—and a concern for economists as well as environmentalists. Two economists with Resources for the Future, Robert U. Ayres and Allen V. Kneese, estimate in fact that it would not be surprising if the unaccounted spillover costs of industrial waste alone ran into the tens of billions of dollars annually.

Not only are such spillovers left out of the prices people pay, they are absent from or misrepresented in the arithmetic of national income accounts, including that grand compilation of nearly all transactions in the economy—the Gross National Product. The GNP is, in effect, the sum of goods and services produced in the economy, but it neglects to subtract the bads and disservices. If anything, bads are often counted as a plus; medical costs due to air pollution, for instance, increase the GNP. The distortion is central to the emerging doubts of Mishan and other economists about growth, GNP-style, as a desirable goal of economic activity. A measure that properly took into account the bads, the spillovers, Mishan feels, might very well show that we have not moved ahead at all in recent decades—not in terms of social and personal contentment—in spite of our ardent and vastly consumptive pursuit of happiness.

This is a repeated theme in Mishan's writing and utterances, and he offers several more or less technical variations on it. One of the essential justifications of economic "growthmania"—as Mishan terms the preoccupation with growth—is that more production means more choices for consumers, which in the philosophy of economics is almost self-evidently a good thing. But Mishan questions that growth is actually expanding choice, contending that spillover in Western postwar economies subtracts more choices than increased production adds. In his *Technology and Growth: The Price We Pay*, Mishan put it this way:

As the carpet of "increased choice" is being unrolled before us by the foot, it is simultaneously being rolled up behind us by the yard. . . . In all that contributes in trivial ways to his ultimate satisfaction, the things at which modern business excels, new models of cars and transistors, prepared foodstuffs and plastic *objets d'art*, man has ample choice. In all that destroys his enjoyment of life, he has none.

Some economists are not so sure that national economic measurements could be improved. Professors James Tobin and William Nordhaus at Yale recently came up with a

study that calculated that well-being is growing at least as
fast as the GNP, possibly faster. But Mishan dismisses such
calculations almost out of hand.

I feel like Cobbett [William Cobbett, the late eighteenth and
early nineteenth century English political writer] when he was
riding around England and complaining about them putting
sheep all over the place and throwing the farmers out of work.
And people would produce statistics saying this isn't so. He re-
plied, "What do I care for statistics? Can I not see with my own
eyes?" And I feel very much the same way. Don't quote me statistics. I go around and see things. I notice the air is foul, people
are tense, crime is rising, people are unsure of themselves. And you
can just notice these things everywhere.

Well-Being on the Skids

Things were not as bad, he insists, before the postwar
spurt of growth.

I was in England after I graduated from Chicago in 1951. We
were still on the ration in 1951 and if you compare the GNP in
Britain then, per capita, with that of the United States today, I
would say today it's at least four or five times as high. Is anybody
seriously going to say that people are five times as happy as they
were then, or even happier? There was a general sense of contentment and serenity which you do not meet in the United States
today. So much for GNP.

Mishan does not stand alone, however, in thinking that
economic "growth" has actually amounted to a shrinkage in
terms of real well-being. A recent Harris poll, for example,
asked people to compare the United States as "a place to
live" now against a decade ago. The results: 43 percent of
the respondents think life has "gotten worse," only 30 percent thought better, the remaining 24 percent thought nothing much had changed. Even President Nixon, who has
been an almost relentlessly positive thinker about the American way of life, said in his State of the Union address . . .
[January 22, 1970]: "Never has a nation seemed to have more
and enjoyed it less."

Still, Mishan's blunt pronouncements along these lines,
stripped of academic caution and unaccompanied by rigor-

ous social-science "empiricism," have raised some eyebrows
in academia, as have other of Mishan's less restrained utterances. The preeminent figure of modern economics, John
Maynard Keynes, was not much more "scientific" than is
Mishan in terms of his concern for analyzing data. Yet
Mishan can thank his reputation in more traditional economic analysis for his survival; a lesser economist would
have been booted out the back door of the academy long ago
for his untempered and unscientific assaults on established
thinking—as the American economist with whom Mishan
is most frequently compared, John Kenneth Galbraith,
almost was.

Like Galbraith, Mishan is found guilty in some academic
circles of journalistic oversimplification (Mishan once
wanted to be a journalist, he confesses) and lack of sufficient
objectivity. Galbraith and Mishan have taken aim at many
of the same targets in economic policy-making, too. But there
are decided differences between the two men. In particular,
Mishan is more specifically concerned with—and about—economic growth than Galbraith. "Galbraith," noted Mishan
in a preface to his *Costs of Economic Growth,* "appeared to
be optimistic about the potential growth in an affluent society. No sign of any such optimism about the future will be
found lurking in any corner of this essay."

As a personality, Mishan is also a decidedly more private
and less conventional person than Galbraith; it is hard to
imagine him as a major political or diplomatic figure. A
fellow graduate-student at Chicago remembers Mishan
twenty years ago as already being a "confirmed eccentric and
health bug." He insisted on twelve hours of sleep in a room
muffled from sound, refused to wear a topcoat in bitter-cold
Chicago winters and took to jogging long before it was the
fashion.

Mishan, at fifty-three, still lifts weights; he is an amateur
sculptor, and he personally suffers, one imagines, many of
the indignities and discomforts that he finds modern Western
societies creating for themselves. A father of four, he lives in

the pleasant residential community of Dormans Park, about an hour and a half from downtown London.

Mishan's crankiness, and a tendency to intellectually irritate even many of those who generally agree with him, may account, one leading American economist feels, for the fact that he is still a "reader"—somewhat higher than an associate professor in America—instead of a full professor at the London School of Economics.

In fact, Mishan may be more highly regarded as prophet these days outside his own land. He has been embraced, in part at least, by liberal-to-radical thinkers in the United States who share his doubts about a growth-directed economy, even if they are skeptical of Mishan's yearning for bygone ways. A somewhat radical group of economists was responsible for hiring him to teach at American University. "We thought Mishan was raising important questions about the most basic assumptions of our economic system," says economics department head Charles Wilbur.

What Kind of Future?

In one of our discussions with him, he said:

The question now is what kind of future do we want. Are we going to imagine the future as this chap Toffler does in *Future Shock*, as something that's speeding toward us and something toward which we have to adapt if we are to survive, or are we to consider it something that we ourselves make—that time doesn't really move for that matter, that we move through time, and can move at our own pace. Are we going to choose the future, and if so are we going to choose the kind of life with a lot of scientific innovation going on, and for what purpose is this? These are questions that one can ask.

In choosing our future, Mishan, like a growing number of social scientists, feels we should develop measurements that reach more deeply into societal well-being than do national income figures; that we need such measurements as guides to where we've been and where we're heading. But according to F. Thomas Juster of the National Bureau of Economic Research, it may take a decade of work to expand the GNP concept into a measurement befitting the late twentieth century, and Mishan is impatient with such prospects. "Once the econometricians get a vested interest in measuring these things," he charges, "they'll call for more and more money to develop newer and newer techniques. And while they try to find ideal solutions, the problems will remain unsolved."

Rather, he outlines, somewhat sketchily, two approaches dealing with spillovers that need not wait until the numbers are in. The more modest of the two is to set up separate areas where specified disamenities of modern life are excluded: "people preserves," he has called them. As a possible beginning, he proposes making a number of large residential areas off-limits to motorized traffic or airplane flyovers. He sees New York City's experiments with carless streets as a baby step in this direction, and he points out that there are other existing precedents in such things as no-smoking cars and separate facilities for men and women. Let the car-lovers have their own areas too if they want them, says the car-hater. "Motoring enthusiasts could pursue their pastime unobstructed by speed limits and dwell together in roaring harmony."

A more profound and perhaps more difficult solution to disamenities and illfares that Mishan proposes is a Bill of Amenity Rights that would guarantee individuals' privacy, clean air, quiet and clean water, and would oblige anyone infringing on such rights either to purchase the affected individuals' permission to do so, or to cease infringing. Individuals and companies would, in effect, pay their spillover costs. For instance, an airline company, Mishan explains,

would have the option of continuing all its services provided completely effective antinoise devices were installed, or, to the extent they were not completely effective, of paying full compensation for all the residual noise thrown on to the public. Under such a dispensation, the costs of operating the Concorde over Britain would have to include compensation for inflicting on us a plague of sonic booms. As an economic proposition it would be a dead duck.

And deservedly so, as a social proposition, Mishan clearly feels.

Far from being a novel incursion of law, Mishan sees the case for amenity rights as being

no different in kind from those used in defense of men's right to private property. . . . With respect to equity, it is a cardinal liberal tenet that every man should be allowed the freedom to pursue his own interest provided that in doing so he inflicts no harm on others. The postwar eruption of environmental spillovers forms a classic instance of the most blatant infringement of this crucial proviso, an instance, that is, of severe and growing damage to the welfare of innocent people as a by-product of the pursuit by others of profit or pleasure, for which damage there is at present no legal redress of any value.

Within the legal framework of amenity rights, moreover, Mishan sees the economic system handling spillovers without constant government attention. Mishan describes himself as a pragmatist as far as economic polity goes; he shuns, he says, doctrinaire economic systems preferred by both Left and Right, including the free-enterprise purism of his former thesis adviser, Milton Friedman. Yet, he seems to lean toward free enterprise rather than the direct government regulation and policing that many environmentalists pose as the answer to industrial pollution. "Simply change the law from being permissive of spillovers to being prohibitive of them," he writes, "and the justly admired market mechanism will tend to a solution that seeks to avoid spillovers." Products would disappear or be replaced by ones more in line with modern amenity demands. There would be a booming market, presumably, for noiseless cars, silent saws, even, perhaps, a return of the push lawnmower, propelled by people who give up electric exercising machines, as the collected spillover costs of electricity production pushes utility rates up.

From Contempt to Concern

Mishan has been concerned about the economic problems of growth since 1956 when he joined the faculty of the London School of Economics, and he has been pondering them

aloud since 1958. That year, he addressed an economics society at the LSE on the problems of growth and, he recalls,
"met with the most dreadful response. I was made the object
of ridicule, contempt was hurled upon me. 'How can you
doubt this, you must be mad.' But now everybody's willing
to talk about such matters, everybody's concerned with them
now."

Indeed, a number of areas in the United States, including
the state of Oregon, have recently turned inhospitable to
growth. Instead of traditional come-hither boosterism, these
areas have begun making it clear that they don't want any
more industry or people. A growing number of young people
evidently attach as little value to the "baubles" of modern
industry as Mishan does and are seeking, at least momen-
tarily, less encumbered forms of life. And Congress, in its
political wisdom, saw fit to vote down a yet bigger, faster
(and noisier) airplane.

Of course, not everyone agrees with Mishan's objections,
conclusions and proposals. In fact, economic growth is still
hailed and pursued as a national goal of virtually self-evident
worthiness. The faithful still include United States policy-
makers. When the United States last year reached an estimated $1 trillion Gross National Product, President Nixon
celebrated this impressively large and round number by asserting that a large and growing economy was vital to such
national goals as maintaining a viable, pleasant environment,
cleaning up crime and urban decay, improving the quality
of goods and services and reducing poverty.

Something of an anti-antigrowth argument seems to be
crystallizing these days. It acknowledges, somewhat defen-
sively, that we have not reached utopia yet, but claims that
in the balance most people are better off than they would
be without the spur of economic and technological development of the last several decades; and that if there are problems, more growth, rather than less, is the necessary solution.
One of the more compelling objections to a no-growth or
slow-growth economy is put forward, as Mr. Nixon did it, in

terms of society's underclasses. Only a rapidly expanding economy, say some economists and politicians, can hope to eradicate poverty. Critics of Mishan complain that his concerns about growth are focused on essentially middle-class, even upper-middle-class, niceties.

Not at all, Mishan replies.

> I've said so many times that what I'm concerned with is the ordinary common man [he told us]. I want to extend choice to him. I'm not concerned with the professional people, the scientists, etc. In the future they envisage, they will have some sort of consolation. . . . The wealthy can always get away [from disamenities].

But aren't poorer people's incomes likely to move up if average income is rising?

> Yes, that tends to happen [he said]. But I don't know how much consolation that gives you really. I think it was Toynbee who said the worst country to be poor in is America. And by poor, he meant poor in a way that Americans are poor. It's always with mortification that we have to read that the poverty line here is $3,500 or something, which in England is consistently above the average pay. But here in America, the poor person seems to have needs—needs, mind you—which are not needs in other countries. The poor have more in this country, but they don't feel any better.

The current American recession has been defined in part by a fall-off in the rate of growth of the GNP, and in part by an increase in what has come to be an almost as carefully regarded barometer—the unemployment rate. Some economists say that high growth and low unemployment are intertwined. But Mishan made it clear that he is not one of them. "You can have a stationary economy in which expenditure is high and there is practically no unemployment and you can have a growing economy in which unemployment is high," he said. But in United States experience, at least, a low economic growth rate has tended to be accompanied by high unemployment, the situation we are experiencing today.

The plastic baubles and near-rubbish to which, in Mishan's view, so much of our production is devoted may produce little satisfaction or enrichment to consumers, but at least they provide jobs for producers. Did Mishan find any redeeming social virtue in such arguments?

Predictably not. If we want to keep people working as much as they are, there is a lot more worthy work to be done, he suggested.

> You can always maintain the same employment if you're willing to produce different things. There's plenty of manpower, for example, that can be put into remodeling your cities to make them more livable. . . . I don't think there'd be any shortage of ways of maintaining employment. On the other hand, if there were, there's nothing that says we couldn't produce less goods and take up more leisure. That option is always open.

Mishan acknowledges that in the short run at least, any changes in the types of production or nonproduction (in the case of expanded leisure time) would be no easy or painless matter.

> No change can be made without some disruption of some kind. The question always is, Is it worth it. I think it is worth it. The path we're on is so intolerable, so suffocating, that it's worth putting up with a year or two of inconvenience to rearrange matters.

Nearly all of Mishan's analysis and doubts about the direction of modern economies are focused on Western countries. What about the rest of the world? If ours are over-developed economies in some sense, we asked him, did he think the world's underdeveloped countries should try to expand their economies, and should we help them or should they stop where they are?

> That's a question I hate to discuss [he said, but he did]. One of the reasons I don't like to discuss the underdeveloped countries is because so many people get furious when you suggest that they should have a different thing, which they regard as inferior—that we should have all the high-powered stuff and they should be content with the spinning wheel and hand loom.

Was Mishan, in fact, suggesting as much?

> Suppose I were dictator of India or something like that. I certainly wouldn't follow in the footsteps of the West. I'd like to

develop small industry. If we could leave aside defense and the nuclear age, I'd certainly try to follow much more in the steps of Gandhi—trying to keep population down, trying to spread industry over the country generally, not to keep it in a few places, not to imitate the West, not to have prestige projects. Self-sufficiency is what I'd aim for, and just a sensible standard of life. Now this can be done with much less capital than in the United States, much less than in England for that matter.

Does the desirability of growth depend on how well off a country or a group is? "Certainly," he answered. "When you consider certain parts of South America and you see those shanty towns—I mean I'm concerned with civilization. I don't want to go back to the cave man." At what point, then, does economic and technological development become a problem? He couldn't offer any formula as such, he said.

I don't think you can define it by a single measure. It's almost tautological. It becomes a problem when problems begin to occur, you might say. When spillover effects begin to mount up. There was no problem of water pollution, say, in the eighteenth century. In the nineteenth it began, but you could cope with it. In the twentieth century, well—up to the war, possible, and since then impossible. You can't take a single indicator. It's just turned out that the rapid acceleration since the war has brought a lot of these things together.

But is the technological demon really more threatening today than it has been in times past? Perhaps the most insidious doubt cast on Mishan's critique of the quality of progress is that we have heard it all before, going back to the original Luddites and even earlier. For example, Thomas Jefferson, 1785:

The Europeans value themselves on having subdued the horse to the uses of man, but I doubt whether we have not lost more than we have gained by the use of this animal, for no one has occasioned so much degeneracy of the human body.

We read the quote to Mishan and asked him if his skepticism about technology and growth wasn't in effect to be discounted as one of the patterns of history.

Does one say if you can find a precedent it really isn't happening? [he asked]. . . . Possibly walking was better than riding a horse, and riding a bicycle was worse than riding a horse, and riding a motor car was worse still, and so on. There's nothing paradoxical about it or even ironic. It could be quite true. The country is disappearing. Even in the days of Chaucer, they were talking about the country disappearing, and it was true. But today it really is disappearing, it's disappearing much more.

To Kill the Machine

Did his doubts about growth lead Mishan to favor something like biologist René Dubos's "steady state" society and economy? No, he said, he did not understand how such a thing would work. Besides, he insisted, he is not against growth per se, only the type of growth determined by technology that he feels has been dominant in the West since World War II. He is not against technological change, per se, either, and could see some areas—medicine, for instance— where advances in technology could be beneficial. He could also see, he said, where new technologies could be helpful in undoing the bads of existing technologies—air-filters and engine-silencers, for instance.

But he said and has written that one of the surest and most direct ways to halt the disagreeable side-effects of such technologies is to do away with the offending instruments themselves. Did he really think there was much likelihood that we would? Mishan was equivocal. He said we have become so dependent on the automobile, for instance, our life-styles and communities are so built up around the thing that we would be hard put to abandon it if we wanted to. He owns two cars himself, he confessed. ("But don't worry, as soon as the revolution comes, I'll be only too glad to ditch both of them.") He mentioned his separate-areas and amenity-rights ideas as possible routes out, but did not seem very confident that they would be adopted on a broad scale.

Did he see any hopeful signs? Some, he said. "The voting down of the SST gave me some pleasure. The main hope is that people are now willing to talk about problems of growth." But in conversation, as in his writings, Mishan is almost relentlessly pessimistic about what he ultimately regards as the dull, misguided, avaricious drift of modern man. We talked about one of his most recent and most pessimistic articles, in which he raises the specter of increasing control of society by scientists and technologists. Mishan writes that man can and should control his future, but suggests that it looks pretty unlikely that man is going to exercise this control. We asked if that was a proper interpretation of what he was saying?

Yes [he answered]. Somehow my mind has wandered to *Paradise Lost*, where Milton is arguing passionately that God knows that Adam is going to eat of the apple and is preparing to punish him. And Milton is trying to say that this doesn't mean that Adam doesn't have free will. I felt this was a sophism, because if God knows this is going to happen, then of course Adam hasn't got any free will.

This is the thought that just came to mind when we were talking about this. I think there's a kind of despair on my own part. It's true that people do have the choice, but I think that unless they make some Herculean effort, moral effort, political effort, things are simply going to keep getting worse.

Mishan expressed his ultimate lack of optimism about the likelihood of such an effort arising when he made his parting address at American University.

We fear to jettison our growth ideology [he said], because we can see nothing to replace it, because there is no road back. So we drift on, making a virtue of necessity, calling out for more speed and soothing our apprehensions with technological fantasies.

This was before President Nixon announced *his* new economic policy, with increased automobile production as a major goal on the way to stimulating the economy to greater production, higher employment, a bigger gross national product, a boundless new prosperity.

THE END OF THE "COWBOY ECONOMY"? [3]

In searching for ways to meet the nation's soaring energy needs without damaging the environment, some American experts are beginning to question one of this country's most cherished beliefs: the idea that boundless economic growth is indispensable to the good life.

If the environment is finite, according to these social scientists, engineers, economists and environmentalists, then perhaps economic growth has its limits too, particularly the unbridled growth that has characterized the United States almost from the start.

What those limits are, or more specifically how a slow-growth economy would be managed and what the social and political implications of such a policy of national planning might be, are questions that the critics of growth have given little detailed thought to.

But they agree that the changes needed to contain the energy crisis may well prove to be radical since, if the logic of the situation is carried to its end, whoever sets priorities for energy consumption wields enormous power over the economy and over the entire national life style.

They are convinced, in any case, that change of some sort will be essential. As Dr. Barry Commoner, an outspoken Washington University biologist, asserts: "The environment got there first, and it's up to the economic system to adjust to the environment. Any economic system must be compatible with the environment, or it will not survive."

Controlling growth, economists say, would confront the nation with a host of difficult problems. Unemployment could rise. The poor could be locked in their poverty. Education, research and cultural pursuits might suffer. The nation could lose economic and political stature.

[3] From "Nation's Energy Crisis: Is Unbridled Growth Indispensable to the Good Life?" by John Noble Wilford, staff correspondent. New York *Times*. p 24. Jl. 8, '71. © 1971 by The New York Times Company. Reprinted by permission.

Millions of individual decisions traditionally made through the random choices of consumers and the supply-and-demand forces of a relatively uncontrolled economy would have to be passed upward to the national level and made through some form of comprehensive national planning.

Most authorities agree that such far-reaching Government power would run against the American grain and that the American people would not easily accept more controls unless the energy crisis got much worse. What the critics of growth are saying, in a word, is that the crisis *is* getting worse, and rapidly.

Reexamination Suggested

Consumption of all energy sources is rising between 3 and 4 percent a year, which is faster than population increases and basic economic growth. By the year 2000, according to some projections, there will be 320 million Americans (compared to 203 million now), and they may be using three or four times the current energy output. Hardly a shore or river bank would be without a power plant every few miles.

"We're not pessimists or doom-mongers. We just see technological reasons to do some new social thinking," says Dr. John List, assistant professor of engineering at the California Institute of Technology's new Environmental Quality Laboratory.

We've got about twenty years in which to reorganize [Dr. List continues]. Population growth hardly comes into it at all. It's growth in per capita consumption. It's just plain affluence. The only way out of it that we can see is to curb the energy consumption per person. Not exactly a no-growth situation, but slow it down from this 9 percent [growth-rate] madness.

. . . When slow-growth or no-growth ideas are raised, businessmen, economists and engineers usually react with variations of the time-honored principle that growth is progress and progress is good. They stand firm on the premise reflected by John L. O'Sullivan, the American editor credited with coining the expansionist expression "manifest destiny." Said Mr. O'Sullivan in 1845: "The only healthy state of a nation is perpetual growth."

But a crisis, if not completely catastrophic, can change thinking patterns and give impetus to social invention, as the economic crisis of the Depression years did in this country. To ecologists, such radical thinking is once again a necessity.

One of the basic laws of the biosphere is that energy, when expended, ends up as heat—the warmth of a stove or light bulb, the blast of an industrial furnace, the heat of an auto engine and the heat emitted by power-plant stacks and cooling waters.

In power plants, conventional or nuclear, only 30 to 40 percent of the fuel's heat is converted to electricity, and engineers doubt there can be any significant improvements in efficiency for at least two or three decades. Consequently, some 60 percent of the heat is released in a concentrated dose at the power-plant site and the other 40 percent over the points of use, primarily the urban areas.

At some point, scientists caution, the cumulative effects of power generation could alter global climate.

Cutback Won't Be Easy

Slowing down the rate of increase in energy consumption will not be easy. It would not help much to abolish many of those gadgets of affluence, such as the electric toothbrush or electric carving knife. Each uses less than eight kilowatt hours a year.

The big residential consumers are refrigerators, electric ranges, air conditioners, freezers—all considered necessities by the "haves" and desired objects by the "have-nots." New Yorkers, for example, may not want Con Edison to spoil the Hudson Valley any more with power plants—but they keep buying more air conditioners.

And residential consumption is slightly less than a third of the total. According to the Edison Electric Institute, 41 percent of electricity is consumed by industry, 32 percent residential, 23 percent commercial (stores, shopping centers, office buildings, hospitals, etc.) and 4 percent others (street lights, subways, etc.).

How to slow down growth—through restrictions on energy consumption or reductions in economic development in order to curb energy demand—is something most economists would rather not contemplate. Adam Smith, in *The Wealth of Nations* two centuries ago, summed up their position: "The progressive state is in reality the cheerful and the hearty state to all the different orders of the society. The stationary state is dull; the declining, melancholy."

Some economists, like Yale University's Dr. Henry C. Wallich, dismiss no-growth ideas as "absolute bunk."

They see more unemployment as the most immediate and deplorable effect. According to a "law" worked out by Dr. Arthur Okun, a senior fellow at the Brookings Institution and former economics adviser to President Johnson, the nation's basic economy must grow at a rate of 4 to 4.5 percent annually to absorb the growing labor force and increases in productivity, the output per man-hour. A 1 percent drop in economic growth would thus lead to a one third of 1 percent rise in unemployment.

Any fundamental curbing of energy consumption, economists say, would mean stabilizing the gross national product, the total output of goods and services, which currently runs at an annual rate of slightly more than $1 trillion.

The only remotely realistic way to do that, the economists add, is to reduce the hours people work each week. It would mean asking people to trade added income for more leisure, to sacrifice future increases in their standard of living.

"What are they going to occupy their time with?" Dr. Wallich asks. "Religious contemplation, art, beautiful thoughts?"

The effect this could have on poor people presents a serious problem. Methods often suggested for reducing energy consumption, such as substantial price increases, would hit the poor hardest.

For a person in Harlem or Watts it could make the difference in having air conditioning, or even a fan. More important, it could cost him his job. The increases could also hurt the users of subways and other electric mass-transit operations, but not the people who ride to work in automobiles, which are responsible for great amounts of pollution.

For these reasons, critics often call slow-growth ideas an elitist attitude, which one industry executive described as "I've got mine, Jack, let's stop here."

Critics of the critics, however, say the impact on the poor could be ameliorated through income redistribution and other social legislation. Besides, they say the argument is often used by people who never really gave a second thought to poor people before.

Another argument against curbing energy production is that cleaning up the environment will take more, not less, energy. W. Donham Crawford, president of the Edison Electric Institute, contends:

> If you want to replace the internal-combustion engine with mass transit in our polluted cities, if you want to recycle aluminum and steel cans into useful products, if you are going to try to clean up the sewage and rivers and lakes, if you're going to clean the air, it will take enormous amounts of electricity.

Conflict Over Timing

But the conflict between many economists and ecologists may be over matters of timing and magnitude rather than of principle.

Dr. Walter W. Heller, University of Minnesota professor and former chairman of the Council of Economic Advisers under President Kennedy, says:

> I think of growth as a source of the problem, but also as a solution. We're doing a bad enough job in the face of growth. An

absence of growth would be a corrosive factor in solving our problems. But we must, in time, redirect the proceeds of growth, and
the first claim should be on repairing the ravages of growth.

It is also possible that growth rates will begin to taper
off because of natural economic and cultural forces.

In California, as in many fast-growing states, there is a
shift in construction from single-family homes to multiple
dwellings; an apartment uses about two thirds the electric
power of a single-family house. Lower birth rates will mean
a decrease in the labor force's growth twenty years from now,
and there is already a gradual shift in the labor force from
manufacturing to less power-demanding service and trade
occupations.

Even without additional taxes or surcharges to support
research and to discourage overuse, all forecasters predict
considerably higher costs of energy, perhaps 50 percent increases in the decade. This would be a result of resource
scarcities and the costs of antipollution measures.

And it just may be that there is a saturation point for
human energy needs. How many more cars and air conditioners and appliances can the American middle classes need
or want? Perhaps the consumers' boom will cool off. Perhaps
at some point most growth-in-energy demand will reflect
population gains and the acquisitions of poorer people.

This could bring to an end the exponential growth-
curves that have been the pattern all this century—that is,
the doubling of electricity consumption every ten years. It
has to end sometime, through some natural or willed de-
celeration, because, as Dr. Dennis Gabor, the British technologist, says: "Exponential curves grow to infinity only in
mathematics. In the physical world, they either turn round
and saturate, or they break down catastrophically."

In random but not insignificant ways, Americans are
showing signs of turning away from reflex Chamber-of-
Commerce boosterism to a more selective approach
toward growth.

Cancellation of the supersonic transport was the most dramatic expression of such a questioning attitude. Dr. John Kenneth Galbraith, the Harvard University economist, calls the SST decision "historic" because "for the first time we decided the advantages of a new type of growth were outweighed by the disadvantages."

Similar public protests killed proposals for a jet airport in the Everglades and the Cross-Florida Barge Canal.

Basic Social Issues

But to embark on a conscious policy of curbing growth raises fundamental social questions that go much deeper than the economics of living. They strike at the heart of American ethics and philosophy.

"Up till very recently, man has inhabited, psychologically, a virtually unlimited flat earth," says Dr. Kenneth E. Boulding, a University of Colorado economist, explaining the potential impact of the finite-earth concept on man's thinking.

There has always been somewhere to go over the horizon, some boundary to the known world beyond which there were further worlds to explore. Now this long period of human expansion has suddenly come to an end. We are living in just so big a house and there are only so many things that can be done with it. The psychological impact of this shift has barely begun to be felt.

Advocating a new "ecologic ethic," Dr. Garrett Hardin, professor of biology at the University of California at Santa Barbara, says:

The ethical system under which we operated in the past was possibly adequate for an uncrowded world. But it is not adequate for a world that is already critically overcrowded, a world in which it is increasingly difficult for anyone to do anything at all without seriously affecting the well-being of countless other human beings.

No crisis so complex can be easily solved, but the few ideas being discussed generally involve the types of social innovations that may be necessary to match the nation's technological capabilities. The ideas center on some kind of national energy policy in the broader context of national economic and environmental planning. As a beginning, air and water and other environmental standards are being established on a national basis for the first time.

Writing in the summer [1971] issue of *The American Scholar,* Dr. Peter L. Marks, professor of biology at Cornell University, went so far as to advocate abolishing all state, county and city governments and replacing them "with regional governments based on ecological boundaries," such as a watershed.

Since he joined the General Electric Company last year, Dr. Thomas O. Paine, former head of the National Aeronautics and Space Administration, has initiated a strategic study of the nation's energy situation. The study, which is not yet completed, explores such ideas as regional land-use and water planning, a national energy system of interconnected transmission lines and priorities for resource exploitation and technological development.

These represent the probing first steps as the nation learns to make the transition from what Dr. Boulding of the University of Colorado calls the cowboy economics of unfettered growth to the planned, orderly growth of "spaceship economics," the concept of man's dependence on a finite, enclosed life-support system known as earth.

The energy crisis reflects the difficulty of that transition, the slow weighing of the costs of radical social change against the costs of letting things go unchanged. The crisis also confirms the agonizing truth of Buckminster Fuller's words.

"Now there is one outstandingly important fact regarding Spaceship Earth," Mr. Fuller, the inventor, says, "and that is that no instruction book came with it."

IV. OF COSTS AND PRIORITIES

EDITOR'S INTRODUCTION

The costs of cleaning up our environment (i.e., that of the United States alone) are estimated at upwards of $120 billion over the next ten years. Such expenditures, if made, would no doubt solve some of the aesthetic and health problems facing the nation—foul air, polluted waters, scarred and defaced countryside—but they would not really affect such sensitive and highly controversial issues as the one discussed in the preceding section (economic growth and its limits) or even the problem of limiting human numbers as a means of restoring the environment. In the meantime, however, the problems of immediate costs and priorities are paramount.

The articles in this section are designed to add further depth to our understanding of these immediate problems—baffling, and controversial as they are. Since its heady breakthrough into the public's consciousness about the time of Earth Day, 1970, the environmental movement has shown signs of settling down into a more conservative pattern of activity—a movement seeking to consolidate some of the gains it has already made while pondering new directions. The first article in this section, by the well-known economist and management consultant Peter F. Drucker, reflects this mood. It is a quiet call for environmental activists to choose among and necessarily accept some lesser evils (as between DDT and disease, for example), with the aim of preventing the movement as a whole from running off eccentrically. The next article, from *Fortune* magazine, serves to reinforce such practical advice by enumerating the many obstacles to be overcome and the heavy costs involved in obtaining clean air and clean water.

We are reminded that survival has an international dimension in the third article, taken from *Business Week,* which points up the mounting red tape ready to snarl environmental programs—and international trade relations, for that matter—once countries begin to institute their own quality-control programs tied to environmental considerations. Quite obviously, one priority is a high level of international cooperation if any nation's environment is ultimately to be preserved. In the final article a writer on the staff of *Science* magazine notes the doldrums into which various environmental activist organizations have fallen, the general malaise afflicting the movement, and the reasons why public support of environmentalist goals appears to be faltering.

CHOOSING THE LESSER EVILS [1]

Everybody today is "for the environment." Laws and agencies designed to protect it multiply at all levels of government. Big corporations take full-color ads to explain how they're cleaning up, or at least trying to. Even you as a private citizen probably make some conscientious effort to curb pollution. At the same time, we have learned enough about the problem to make some progress toward restoring a balance between man and nature. The environmental crusade may well become the great cause of the seventies—and not one moment too soon.

Yet the crusade is in real danger of running off the tracks, much like its immediate predecessor, the so-called war on poverty. Paradoxically, the most fervent environmentalists may be among the chief wreckers. Many are confused about the cause of our crisis and the ways in which we might resolve it. They ignore the difficult decisions that must be made; they splinter the resources available for attacking environmental

[1] Article, "Saving the Crusade," by Peter F. Drucker, Clarke Professor of Social Sciences at the Claremont Graduate School, Claremont, California, and visiting lecturer (spring term) at New York University. *Harper's Magazine.* 244: 66-71. Ja. '72. Copyright © 1971, by Minneapolis Star and Tribune Co., Inc. Reprinted from the January 1972 issue of *Harper's Magazine* by permission of the author.

problems. Indeed, some of our leading crusaders seem almost perversely determined to sabotage their cause—and our future.

Consider, for example, the widespread illusion that a clean environment can be obtained by reducing or even abolishing our dependence on technology. The growing pollution crisis does indeed raise fundamental questions about technology—its direction, uses, and future. But the relationship between technology and the environment is hardly as simple as much antitechnological rhetoric would have us believe. The invention that has probably had the greatest environmental impact in the past twenty-five years, for instance, is that seemingly insignificant gadget, the wire-screen window. The wire screen, rather than DDT or antibiotics, detonated the "population explosion" in underdeveloped countries, where only a few decades ago as many as four out of five children died of such insect-borne diseases as "summer diarrhea" or malaria before their fifth birthday. Would even the most ardent environmentalist outlaw the screen window and expose those babies again to the flies?

The truth is that most environmental problems require technological solutions—and dozens of them. To control our biggest water pollutant, human wastes, we will have to draw on all sciences and technologies from biochemistry to thermodynamics. Similarly, we need the most advanced technology for adequate treatment of the effluents that mining and manufacturing spew into the world's waters. It will take even more new technology to repair the damage caused by the third major source of water pollution in this country—the activities of farmers and loggers.

Even the hope of genuine disarmament—and the arms race may be our worst and most dangerous pollutant—rests largely on complex technologies of remote inspection and surveillance. Environmental control, in other words, requires technology at a level at least as high as the technology whose misuse it is designed to correct. The sewage-treatment plants that are urgently needed all over the world will be designed, built, and kept running not by purity of heart, ballads, or Earth Days but by crew-cut engineers working in very large organizations, whether businesses, research labs, or government agencies.

Who Will Pay?

The second and equally dangerous delusion abroad today is the common belief that the cost of cleaning the environment can be paid for out of "business profits." After taxes, the profits of all American businesses in a good year come to $60 billion or $70 billion. And mining and manufacturing —the most polluting industries—account for less than half of this. But at the lowest estimate, the cleanup bill, even for just the most urgent jobs, will be three or four times as large as all business profits.

Consider the most efficient and most profitable electric-power company in the country (and probably in the world): the American Power Company, which operates a number of large power systems in the Midwest and upper South. It has always been far more ecology-minded than most other power companies, including the Government's own TVA. Yet cleaning up American Power's plants to the point where they no longer befoul air and water will require, for many years to come, an annual outlay close to, if not exceeding, the company's present annual profit of $100 million. The added expense caused by giving up strip mining of coal or by reclaiming strip-mined land might double the company's fuel bill, its single largest operating cost. No one can even guess what it would cost—if and when it can be done technologically—to put power transmission lines underground. It might well be a good deal more than power companies have ever earned.

We face an environmental crisis because for too long we have disregarded genuine costs. Now we must raise the costs, in a hurry, to where they should have been all along. The expense must be borne, eventually, by the great mass of the people as consumers and producers. The only choice we have is which of the costs will be borne by the consumer in the form of higher prices, and which by the taxpayer in the form of higher taxes.

It may be possible to convert part of this economic burden into economic opportunity, though not without hard work and, again, new technology. Many industrial or human wastes might be transformed into valuable products. The heat produced in generating electricity might be used in greenhouses and fish farming, or to punch "heat holes" into the layer of cold air over such places as Los Angeles, creating an updraft to draw off the smog. But these are long-range projects. The increased costs are here and now.

Closely related to the fallacy that "profit" can pay the environmental bill is the belief that we can solve the environmental crisis by reducing industrial output. In the highly developed affluent countries of the world, it is true that we may be about to de-emphasize the production-orientation of the past few hundred years. Indeed, the growth sectors of the developed economies are increasingly education, leisure activities, or health care rather than goods. But paradoxical as it may sound, the environmental crisis will force us to return to an emphasis on both growth and industrial output—at least for the next decade.

Overlooked Facts of Life

There are three reasons for this, each adequate in itself.

1. Practically every environmental task demands huge amounts of electrical energy, way beyond anything now available. Sewage treatment is just one example; the difference between the traditional and wholly inadequate methods and a modern treatment plant that gets rid of human and industrial wastes and produces reasonably clear water is primarily electric power, and vast supplies of it. This poses a difficult dilemma. Power plants are themselves polluters. And one of their major pollution hazards, thermal pollution, is something we do not yet know how to handle.

Had we better postpone any serious attack on other environmental tasks until we have solved the pollution problems of electric-power generation? It would be a quixotic decision, but at least it would be a deliberate one. What is simply dishonest is the present hypocrisy that maintains we are serious about these other problems—industrial wastes, for instance, or sewage or pesticides—while we refuse to build the power plants we need to resolve them. I happen to be a member in good standing of the Sierra Club, and I share its concern for the environment. But the Sierra Club's opposition to any new power plant today—and the opposition of other groups to new power plants in other parts of the country (e.g., New York City)—has, in the first place, ensured that other ecological tasks cannot be done effectively for the next five or ten years. Secondly, it has made certain that the internal-combustion engine is going to remain our mainstay in transportation for a long time to come. An electrical automobile or electrified mass transportation—the only feasible alternatives—would require an even more rapid increase in electrical power than any now projected. And thirdly it may well, a few years hence, cause power shortages along the Atlantic Coast, which would mean unheated homes in winter, as well as widespread industrial shutdowns and unemployment. This would almost certainly start a "backlash" against the whole environmental crusade.

2. No matter how desirable a de-emphasis on production might be, the next decade is the wrong time for it in all the developed countries and especially in the United States. The next decade will bring a surge in employment-seekers and in the formation of young families—both the inevitable result of the baby boom of the late forties and early fifties. Young adults need jobs; and unless there is a rapid expansion of jobs in production there will be massive unemployment, especially of low-skilled blacks and other minority group members. In addition to jobs, young families need goods—from housing and furniture to shoes for the baby. Even if the individual family's standard of consumption goes down

quite a bit, total demand—barring only a severe depression—will go up sharply. If this is resisted in the name of ecology, environment will become a dirty word in the political vocabulary.

3. If there is no expansion of output equal to the additional cost of cleaning up the environment, the cost burden will—indeed, must—be met by cutting the funds available for education, health care, or the inner city, thus depriving the poor. It would be nice if the resources we need could come out of defense spending. But of the 6 or 7 percent of our national income that now goes for defense, a large part is cost of past wars, that is, veterans' pensions and disability benefits (which, incidentally, most other countries do not include in their defense budgets—a fact critics of "American militarism" often ignore). Even if we could—or should—cut defense spending, the "peace dividend" is going to be 1 or 2 percent of national income, at best.

But the total national outlay for education (7 to 8 percent), and the inner city and other poverty areas (almost 5 percent) comes to a fifth of total national income today. Unless we raise output and productivity fast enough to offset the added environmental cost, the voters will look to this sector for money. Indeed, in their rejection of school budgets across the nation and in their desperate attempts to cut welfare costs, voters have already begun to do so. That the shift of resources is likely to be accomplished in large part through inflation—essentially at the expense of the lower-income groups—will hardly make the environmental cause more popular with the poor.

The only way to avoid these evils is to expand the economy, probably at a rate of growth on the order of 4 percent a year for the next decade, a higher rate than we have been able to sustain in this country in the postwar years. This undoubtedly entails very great environmental risks. But the alternative is likely to mean no environmental action at all, and a rapid public turn—by no means confined to the "hard hats"—against all environmental concern whatever.

Making Virtue Pay

The final delusion is that the proper way to bring about a clean environment is through punitive legislation. We do need prohibitions and laws forbidding actions that endanger and degrade the environment. But more than that, we need incentives to preserve and improve it.

Punitive laws succeed only if the malefactors are few and the unlawful act is comparatively rare. Whenever the law attempts to prevent or control something everybody is doing, it degenerates into a huge but futile machine of informers, spies, bribe givers, and bribe takers. Today every one of us —in the underdeveloped countries almost as much as in the developed ones—is a polluter. Punitive laws and regulations can force automobile manufacturers to put emission controls into new cars, but they will never be able to force 100 million motorists to maintain this equipment. Yet this is going to be the central task if we are to stop automotive pollution.

What we should do is make it to everyone's advantage to reach environmental goals. And since the roots of the environmental crisis are so largely in economic activity, the incentives will have to be largely economic ones as well. Automobile owners who voluntarily maintain in working order the emission controls of their cars might, for instance, pay a much lower automobile registration fee, while those whose cars fall below accepted standards might pay a much higher fee. And if they were offered a sizable tax incentive, the automobile companies would put all their best energies to work to produce safer and emission-free cars, rather than fight delaying actions against punitive legislation.

Despite all the rhetoric on the campuses, we know by now that capitalism has nothing to do with the ecological crisis, which is fully as severe in the Communist countries. The bathing beaches for fifty miles around Stockholm have become completely unusable, not because of the wicked Swedish capitalists but because of the raw, untreated sewage from Communist Leningrad that drifts across the narrow Baltic. Moscow, even though it still has few automobiles, has as bad an air-pollution problem as Los Angeles—and has done less about it so far.

We should also know that greed has little to do with the environmental crisis. The two main causes are population pressures, especially the pressures of large metropolitan populations, and the desire—a highly commendable one—to bring a decent living at the lowest possible cost to the largest possible number of people.

The environmental crisis is the result of success—success in cutting down the mortality of infants (which has given us the population explosion), success in raising farm output sufficiently to prevent mass famine (which has given us contamination by insecticides, pesticides, and chemical fertilizers), success in getting people out of the noisome tenements of the nineteenth century city and into the greenery and privacy of the single-family home in the suburbs (which has given us urban sprawl and traffic jams). The environmental crisis, in other words, is very largely the result of doing too much of the right sort of thing.

To overcome the problems success always creates, one has to build on it. The first step entails a willingness to take the risks involved in making decisions about complicated and perilous dilemmas:

> What is the best "trade-off" between a cleaner environment and unemployment?
>
> How can we prevent the environmental crusade from becoming a war of the rich against the poor, a new and particularly vicious "white racist imperialism?"
>
> What can we do to harmonize the worldwide needs of the environment with the political and economic needs of other countries, and to keep American leadership from becoming American aggression?
>
> How can we strike the least agonizing balance of risks between environmental damage and mass starvation of poor children, or between environmental damage and large-scale epidemics?

An Environmental Crime?

More than twenty years ago, three young chemical engineers came to seek my advice. They were working for one of the big chemical companies, and its managers had told them to figure out what kind of new plants to put into West Virginia, where poverty was rampant. The three young men had drawn up a long-range plan for systematic job creation, but it included one project about which their top management was very dubious—a ferroalloy plant to be located in the very poorest area where almost everybody was unemployed. It would create 1,500 jobs in a dying small town of 12,000 people and another 800 jobs for unemployed coal miners—clean, healthy, safe jobs, since the new diggings would be strip mines.

But the plant would have to use an already obsolete high-cost process, the only one for which raw materials were locally available. It would therefore be marginal in both costs and product quality. Also the process was a singularly dirty one, and putting in the best available pollution controls would make it even less economical. Yet it was the only plant that could possibly be put in the neediest area. What did I think?

I said, "forget it"—which was, of course, not what the three young men wanted to hear and not the advice they followed.

This, as some readers have undoubtedly recognized, is the prehistory of what has become a notorious "environmental crime," the Union Carbide plant in Marietta, Ohio. When first opened in 1951 the plant was an "environmental pioneer." Its scrubbers captured three quarters of the particles spewed out by the smelting furnaces; the standard at the time was half of that or less. Its smokestacks suppressed more fly ash than those of any other power plant then built, and so on.

But within ten years the plant had become an unbearable polluter to Vienna, West Virginia, the small town across the river whose unemployment it was built to relieve. And for the last five years the town and Union Carbide fought like wildcats. In the end Union Carbide lost. But while finally accepting Federal and state orders to clean up an extremely dirty process, it also announced that it would have to lay off half the 1,500 men now working in the plant—and that's half the people employed in Vienna. The switch to cleaner coal (not to mention the abandonment of strip mining) would also put an end to the 800 or so coal-mining jobs in the poverty hollows of the back country.

There are scores of Viennas around the nation, where marginal plants are kept running precisely because they are the main or only employer in a depressed or decaying area. Should an uneconomical plant shut down, dumping its workers on the welfare rolls? Should the plant be subsidized (which would clearly open the way for everybody to put his hand in the public till)? Should environmental standards be disregarded or their application postponed in "hardship" cases?

If concern for the environment comes to be seen as an attack on the livelihood of workers, public sympathy and political support for it is likely to vanish. It is not too fanciful to anticipate, only a few years hence, the New (if aging) Left, the concerned kids on the campus, and the ministers in a protest march against "ecology" and in support of "the victims of bourgeois environmentalism."

Third World Ecology

In the poor, developing countries where men must struggle to make even a little progress in their fight against misery, any industry bears a heavy burden of high costs and low productivity. Burdening it further with the cost of environmental control might destroy it. Moreover, development in these countries—regardless of their political creed or social organization, in Mao's as well as in Chiang Kai-shek's China and in North as well as in South Vietnam—cannot occur without the four biggest ecological villains: a rapid increase in electric power, chemical fertilizers and pesticides, the automobile, and the large steel mill.

That poor countries regard those villains as economic saviors confronts us with hard political choices. Should we help such countries get what they want (industrialization), or what we think the world needs (less pollution)? How do we avoid the charge, in either case, that our help is "imperialistic?" To complicate matters, there is a looming conflict between environmental concern and national sovereignty. The environment knows no national boundaries. Just as the smog of England befouls the air of Norway, so the chemical wastes of the French potash mines in Alsace destroy the fish of the lower Rhine in Belgium and Holland.

No matter what the statistics bandied about today, the United States is not the world's foremost polluter. Japan holds this dubious honor by a good margin. No American city can truly compete in air pollution with Tokyo, Milan, Budapest, Moscow, or Düsseldorf. No American river is as much of an open sewer as the lower Rhine, the Seine, or the rivers of the industrial Ukraine such as the lower Dnieper. And we are sheer amateurs in littering highways compared to the Italians, Danes, Germans, French, Swedes, Swiss, and Austrians—although the Japanese, especially in littering mountainsides and camp grounds, are clearly even more "advanced."

If not the worst polluter, however, the United States is clearly the largest one. More important, as the most affluent, most advanced, and biggest of the industrial countries, it is expected to set an example. If we do not launch the environmental crusade, no one else will.

We shall have to make sure, however, that other nations join with us. In the absence of international treaties and regulations, some countries—especially those with protectionist traditions, such as Japan, France, and even the United States—may be tempted to impose ecological standards on imports more severe than those they demand of their own producers. On the other hand, countries heavily dependent on exports, especially in Africa and Latin America, may try to gain a competitive advantage by lax enforcement of environmental standards.

One solution might be action by the United Nations to fix uniform rules obliging all its members to protect the environment; and such action is, in fact, now under official study. The United States might help by changing its import regulations to keep out goods produced by flagrant polluters —allowing ample time for countries with severe poverty and unemployment problems to get the cleanup under way. We have good precedent for such an approach in our own history. Forty years ago we halted the evils of child labor by forbidding the transportation in interstate commerce of goods produced by children.

Such a course, however, will demand extraordinary judgment. Unless we persuade other nations to join with us—and set an example ourselves—we may well be accused of trying again to police the world.

Choosing the Lesser Evils

The hardest decisions ahead are even more unprecedented than those we have been discussing. What risks can we afford to take with the environment, and what risks can we *not* afford to take? What are the feasible trade-offs between man's various needs for survival?

Today, for example, no safe pesticides exist, nor are any in sight. We may ban DDT, but all the substitutes so far developed have highly undesirable properties. Yet if we try to do without pesticides altogether, we shall invite massive hazards of disease and starvation the world over. In Ceylon, where malaria was once endemic, it was almost wiped out by large-scale use of DDT; but in only a few years since spraying was halted, the country has suffered an almost explosive resurgence of the disease. In other tropical countries, warns the UN Food and Agriculture Organization, children are threatened with famine, because of insect and blight damage to crops resulting from restrictions on spraying.

Similarly, anyone who has lately traveled the New England turnpike will have noticed whole forests defoliated by the gypsy moth, now that we have stopped aerial spraying.

What is the right trade-off between the health hazard to some women taking the pill and the risk of death to others from abortions? How do we balance the thermal and radiation dangers of nuclear power plants against the need for more electricity to fight other kinds of pollution? How should we choose between growing more food for the world's fast-multiplying millions and the banning of fertilizers that pollute streams, lakes, and oceans?

Such decisions should not be demanded of human beings. None of the great religions offers guidance. Neither do the modern "isms," from Maoism to the anarchism popular with the young. The ecological crisis forces man to play God. Despite the fact that we are unequal to the task, we can't avoid it: the risks inherent in refusing to tackle these problems are the greatest of all. We have to try, somehow, to choose some combination of lesser evils; doing nothing invites even greater catastrophe.

Where to Start

Cleaning up the environment requires determined, sustained effort with clear targets and deadlines. It requires, above all, concentration of effort. Up to now we have had almost complete diffusion. We have tried to do a little bit of everything—and tried to do it in the headlines—when what we ought to do first is draw up a list of priorities in their proper order.

First on such a list belong a few small but clearly definable and highly visible tasks that can be done fairly fast without tying up important resources. Removing the hazard of lead poisoning in old slum tenements might be such an action priority. What to do is well known: burn off the old paint. A substantial number of underemployed black adolescents could be easily recruited to do it.

Once visible successes have been achieved, the real task of priority-setting begins. Then one asks: (1) what are the biggest problems that we know how to solve; and (2) what are the really big ones that we don't know how to solve yet? Clean air should probably head the first list. It's a worldwide problem, and getting worse. We don't know all the answers, but we do have the technological competence to handle most of the problems of foul air today. Within ten years we should have real results to show for our efforts.

Within ten years, too, we should get major results in cleaning up the water around big industrial cities and we should have slowed (if not stopped) the massive pollution of the oceans, especially in the waters near our coastal cities.

As for research priorities, I suggest that the first is to develop birth-control methods that are cheaper, more effective, and more acceptable to people of all cultures than anything we now have. Secondly, we need to learn how to produce electric energy without thermal pollution. A third priority is to devise ways of raising crops for a rapidly growing world population without at the same time doing irreversible ecological damage through pesticides, herbicides, and chemical fertilizers.

Until we get the answers, I think we had better keep on building power plants and growing food with the help of fertilizers and such insect-controlling chemicals as we now have. The risks are now well known, thanks to the environmentalists. If they had not created a widespread public awareness of the ecological crisis, we wouldn't stand a chance. But such awareness by itself is not enough. Flaming manifestoes and prophecies of doom are no longer much help, and a search for scapegoats can only make matters worse.

What we now need is a coherent, long-range program of action, and education of the public and our lawmakers about the steps necessary to carry it out. We must recognize—and we need the help of environmentalists in this task—that we can't do everything at once; that painful choices have to be made, as soon as possible, about what we should tackle first; and that every decision is going to involve high risks and costs, in money and in human lives. Often these will have to be decisions of conscience as well as economics. Is it better, for example, to risk famine or to risk global pollution of earth and water? Any course we adopt will involve a good deal of experimentation—and that means there will be some failures. Any course also will demand sacrifices, often from those least able to bear them: the poor, the unskilled, and the underdeveloped countries. To succeed, the environmental crusade needs support from all major groups in our society, and the mobilization of all our resources, material and intellectual, for years of hard, slow, and often discouraging effort. Otherwise it will not only fail; it will, in the process, splinter domestic and international societies into warring factions.

Now that they have succeeded in awakening us to our ecological peril, I hope the environmentalists will turn their energies to the second and harder task: educating the public to accept the choices we must face, and to sustain a worldwide effort to carry through on the resulting decisions. The time for sensations and manifestos is about over; now we need rigorous analysis, united effort, and very hard work.

SOME COST CONSIDERATIONS [2]

Cleaning up this country's air and water will be a much tougher, slower, and costlier job than politicians and environmentalists sometimes make it sound. Enforcement of strict new legislation will speed up the process, but legislation or public pressures alone aren't enough. Without advances in technology, the big cleanup can only plod along at best. And there are serious lags in new pollution-control technology, as well as in the readiness of business, government, and the public to encourage, apply, and pay for tech-

[2] From "The Long, Littered Path to Clean Air and Water," by Gene Bylinsky, associate editor. *Fortune.* 82:112-15+. O. '70. Reprinted from the October 1970 issue of *Fortune* Magazine by special permission; © 1970 Time Inc.

nological improvements. Recent years have seen advances, to be sure, but the accomplishments only show how much more needs to be done.

Consider, for example, some of the complexities involved in taming the emissions from the internal-combustion engine. To start with, an average automobile yields one quarter to one half a *ton* of carbon monoxide and hydrocarbons a year. It also belches nitrogen oxides, lead compounds, sulfur oxides, and particulate matter. The gleaming, streamlined modern car does not *look* like that kind of polluter. Most of the gases it emits are invisible at street level. But latest estimates—for 1968—show automobiles accounting for about half the nation's yearly total of nearly 200 million tons of air pollutants.

Significant progress in cleaning up the internal-combustion engine has been achieved, and the auto makers have been pouting about what they feel has been a lack of recognition of their efforts. Lynn Townsend, chairman of Chrysler Corporation, said recently: "This accomplishment—at least outside of Detroit—may be the best-kept secret of the 1960s." Still, it's only a beginning.

Up till now, the auto makers have relied mainly on mechanical adjustments to make the car less of a polluter. They began by largely eliminating emission of hydrocarbons from the crankcase, starting with the 1963 models. This was accomplished by the so-called positive crankcase ventilation system that recycles gases to the engine intake. Crankcase blow-by gases are believed to account for 20 or 25 percent of total hydrocarbons emitted by automotive engines. To meet the Federal standards established for 1968 models for hydrocarbons and carbon monoxide, the auto makers redesigned the combustion chambers and adjusted fuel-air ratios and other variables. Recent tests by the National Air Pollution Control Administration on 1970 model cars have shown that all together this tinkering with the engine has eliminated 69 percent of the hydrocarbons and 60 percent of the carbon monoxide, compared with pre-1968 vehicles. These reductions were somewhat below the prescribed standards. So the Federal authorities have now deferred the percentage reductions originally required for 1970 cars to 1972 models.

As the pollution-control administration noted recently, the effect of current emission standards will be canceled out as time goes by. For one thing, the number of cars and the use per car keep growing. "In another decade," says a report from the agency, "these trends will more than offset the effect of the national standards established thus far. Then, total emissions of carbon monoxide and hydrocarbons will again begin to rise."

To prevent that from happening, Federal authorities will be setting ever higher standards. By 1975, for example, they expect to achieve reductions of 97 percent in hydrocarbons and 91 percent in carbon monoxide from emission levels of cars made before 1968. Standards will be set, too, for motor-vehicle pollutants not now covered, such as particulate matter and nitrogen oxides. (Together with hydrocarbons, nitrogen oxides are the principal ingredient of photochemical smog.) Some legislators are impatient with this step-by-step toughening of Federal standards. They want Detroit to move much faster. For example, Senator Edmund Muskie has proposed that the Government halt sales of new cars on January 1, 1975, if the auto makers have not eliminated 90 percent of the exhaust pollutants allowed in 1970 cars.

Something New Under the Hood

Whether the Muskie bill passes or not, meeting the 1975 standards will mean that auto manufacturers will have to equip all cars with either an exhaust-manifold thermal reactor or a catalytic converter. These devices promote the oxidation of carbon monoxide to carbon dioxide (as harmless as bubbles in soda pop) and of hydrocarbons to carbon dioxide and water. Both devices are still under development. A shift to unleaded gasoline might help because both mechanisms can be damaged or deactivated by compounds of lead in the gasoline. President Nixon has recommended a special tax on leaded gasoline and auto manufacturers have announced that most 1971 models have been designated to operate on gasoline with 80 percent less lead. Oil companies are now marketing gasoline with reduced lead content.

Something else has been added to most of the 1971 model cars—a small, elongated canister filled with activated carbon. The canister, located under the hood, will collect gasoline vapors from the carburetor and the gas tank when the car engine is turned off. When the engine is started, fresh air will strip the vapors from the charcoal and they will be burned in the engine. Chrysler Corporation has adopted a different system, using the crankcase to store the vapors. These techniques, already in use on 1970 models sold in California, will reduce total hydrocarbon emissions by another 15 to 20 percent.

One of the troublesome complexities encountered in environmental quality control is that a reduction in one kind of pollutant sometimes entails an increase in another kind of pollutant. Engineers trying to clean up the internal-combustion engine confront a particularly devilish dilemma: in raising combustion temperature to curb hydrocarbon and carbon monoxide emissions, they increase generation of nitrogen oxides. The most important of these, nitrogen dioxide, is toxic in high concentrations. One effective way to dispose of nitrogen dioxide is to decompose it into nitrogen and oxygen. Possibly this could be accomplished with catalysts made of a noble metal such as platinum, obviously an expensive catalyst.

The Pittsburgh Activated Carbon division of Calgon Corporation has tried to remove most of the nitrogen oxides with activated carbon, but hot exhaust gases slowly consume the carbon, melting it "like an ice cube," reports market development manager Donald Tiggelbeck. Tests are continuing, however, Conceivably, activated carbon might work if peak exhaust temperatures of 800° to 1,300° Fahrenheit are reduced by a few hundred degrees. Another possibility is to recycle part of the exhaust gas into the engine to reduce combustion temperature and amounts of nitric oxide formed. None of the methods under investigation, however, is far enough advanced for mass application. As of now, engine modification is the only widely applicable approach.

Some Detroit engineers are unhappy about the tough Federal standards proposed for 1975. For example, Charles M. Heinen, Chrysler's chief engineer for emission control and chemical development, has criticized the Department of Health, Education, and Welfare for going "out on a limb thinking that auto industry engineers or somebody would be able to come up with a technical miracle to make the standards come true." Heinen added: "We earnestly hope we can. We're doing our best. But there is the possibility that we may not overcome the severe technical problems that need to be solved."

Among these problems Heinen cites lack of materials that can withstand high exhaust temperatures and the consequent inability, so far, to devise exhaust-control mechanisms that would last over a car's lifetime. Furthermore, Heinen argues that costs of meeting the 1975 standards would be "staggering." He says the cost of emission-control devices could run as high as $300 per car. (The cost of controls so far has amounted to about $80 per car.) Because many of the proposed devices operate on a rich gasoline mixture, adds Heinen, motorists would use more gasoline. "The reduction in gas mileage on cars could range from 5 to 15 percent." For the nation as a whole, Heinen estimates the costs of meeting the 1975 standards to be $65 *billion* over fifteen years, on the assumptions that at least 150 million vehicles would have to be equipped with advanced control devices by 1990 and that their gasoline consumption would amount to 800 billion gallons between 1975 and 1990.

The effectiveness of all the existing and proposed emission-control mechanisms will depend a lot on how well individual motorists maintain the devices and the engines.

Whether this will work without stringent and frequent inspections is questionable. Heinen points out that one dead spark plug can increase pollutants as much as fifteenfold. "A spark plug misfiring can double the output of hydrocarbons. A carburetor set for too rich an air-fuel mixture can increase carbon monoxide by 50 percent or more." Even the best-intentioned motorist might be contributing to pollution without knowing it—a malfunction in the catalytic muffler, for instance, could not be detected without instruments capable of measuring colorless, odorless gases such as carbon monoxide.

Another Kind of Engine, Perhaps

Some authorities think that a noticeable improvement in the quality of our air could be achieved fairly rapidly if all pre-1968 cars—two thirds of the total automobile population—were equipped with emission-control systems. "You would see a significant reduction in smog in Los Angeles and other big cities," says an official of the National Air Pollution Control Administration. . . . [In 1970] Chrysler and General Motors . . . made available cleaner-air kits for cars and light trucks manufactured between 1955 and 1967, and Ford Motor Company plans to introduce its kit soon. The devices cut hydrocarbon emissions by about 50 percent, carbon monoxide by 35 to 50 percent, and nitrogen oxides by 30 percent. But the motorists' response has been far from enthusiastic. Chrysler so far has sold fewer than ten thousand kits, which cost $20 to buy and install. General Motors, after unsuccessful market tests of its similarly priced kit in Phoenix (only 528 were sold), has not decided whether to offer it nationwide.

So far there is no legal requirement anywhere for motorists to install the kits, although California will make installation mandatory as soon as a kit is certified as being compatible with 75 percent of the pre-1968 cars registered in the state. But even then the impact on air quality will be felt very slowly because the devices will be installed not on all the cars at once but only when they change hands.

In the event that the cleanup of the internal-combustion engine falls short, the Government wants to have an alternative engine developed five years from now. The Nixon Administration is committed to developing one and recently announced the formal start of a program to achieve that end. A large number of alternatives are being looked at, but the gas turbine appears at this point to be the best prospect. Big obstacles to overcome are the turbine's excessive emission of nitrogen oxides and the need for expensive metal replacement parts because of high operating temperatures.

Even if an acceptable turbine or other type of engine emerged soon, the auto makers say, it would take about eight years to tool up for mass production. Another two to four years would pass before the new engine made any significant impact on air pollution. This time-prospect would seem to be reason enough to continue cleaning up the internal-combustion engine.

The second big source of air pollution is industry, particularly power plants that burn fossil fuel. (Nuclear power plants, aside from radioactive emissions, contribute to thermal pollution of water.) Industry generates a substantial share of the five main categories of air pollutants: carbon monoxide, hydrocarbons, sulfur oxides, nitrogen oxides, and particles.

Right now the states are in the process of setting up programs to enforce standards based on national criteria for sulfur dioxide and particulate matter. Those two were selected as a starter by the national air-pollution agency, which has since then issued criteria for carbon monoxide, hydrocarbons, and photochemical oxidants. It will subsequently suggest criteria for other pollutants such as lead and oxides of nitrogen.

The Most Troubling Pollutant

There is no lack of technology today to control particulate matter. Technology has been here for about sixty years and control is mainly a matter of establishing rules and enforcing them. Electrostatic precipitators, mechanical collectors, wet scrubbers, and large filters called bag houses are all old and well-developed devices. With precipitators, for example, 99.8 percent of the particles can be removed from stack gas.

The estimated 21 million tons of particulate matter that will pour into the air over the United States this year could be cut down dramatically to 13 million tons by 1980 if currently available control devices were installed on all sources, according to scientists at the Midwest Research Institute in Kansas City, Missouri. And it now appears that the procrastination in which some industrial managements engaged in the past will no longer be tolerated.

Technology becomes a stumbling block, however, where the more serious gaseous pollutants are concerned. Sulfur dioxide arouses greater anxiety than nitrogen oxides, mainly because more of it is emitted. This colorless gas with a choking, penetrating smell is believed to be largely responsible for sharply rising rates in respiratory ailments among people living in large cities and in industrial areas. As sulfuric acid mist it can harm human lungs, and it has been implicated in major air-pollution disasters.

Since the electric-power generating industry puts forth more than half of the sulfur oxides (17 million of the 33.2 million tons emitted in 1968, latest year for which figures are available), most of the legislative pressures and research efforts have centered on alleviating the SO_2 emissions by power plants. Aggravating the situation is the leaping demand for electricity, together with the slower than expected growth of nuclear power generation. Furthermore, the volume of SO_2 emissions is growing faster than previously estimated. In a report to Congress the National Air Pollution Control Administration recently warned: "There is a widening gap between the rising trend of sulfur oxides emissions and the nation's technological capability for bringing the problem under control." It attributed this lag partly to insufficient

spending on research and development. The report added
that electric-power plants are expected to emit about 43
million tons of sulfur oxides by 1980 if no control measures
are taken. Even with rapid application of the new control
techniques under development, said NAPCA, "It is unlikely
that sulfur dioxide emissions in 1980 will be reduced to
the 1968 level."

The use of low-sulfur fuel has become the principal
means of cutting into SO_2 emissions. Where such fuel is
readily available, substantial progress in reducing SO_2 can
be achieved. In New York City, for example, Consolidated
Edison in 1967 voluntarily switched to coal and oil with
1 percent sulfur content and started burning more natural
gas, which is very low in sulfur. (These measures will cost
the utility $20 million this year. In 1969, New York officially
prescribed fuel with a sulfur content no greater than 1 percent. About 22,000 installations in the city switched from
coal or oil to natural gas or steam. Many large office buildings installed alternative equipment to burn natural gas
when available.

As a result of these measures, New York City air-pollution
control authorities calculate that emissions of SO_2 dropped
56 percent by the end of 1969. To bring the SO_2 down still
further, the city hopes to lower the allowable sulfur content in fuel to 0.3 percent next year. New York still has a
long way to go: despite the recent improvement, its air is
among the worst in the nation in terms of sulfur dioxide
content. The city's goal is reduction to .03 parts per million
or less, a level at which no negative health effects have been
recorded. As of now, at the worst SO_2 spot in the city, on
Manhattan's Lower East Side, concentrations are of the order
of 0.13 ppm.

But supplies of natural gas are limited, and while the
United States has large reserves of low-sulfur coal, most
available deposits are in western states, far from major metropolitan utilities. While coal prices have been moving up,
utility coal can be bought for about $6 a ton. Low-sulfur

coal from distant deposits, however, costs up to an additional $10 a ton for every 1,000 miles it is shipped. Reserves of low-sulfur coal closer to major industrial regions are usually committed to specialized uses—in metallurgy, for example.

Desulfurization of coal and oil is expected to make only a limited contribution to alleviating sulfur oxides. Some of the sulfur can be removed from coal but not quite enough from the standpoint of pollution control. Fuel oil can be desulfurized, and a number of companies are constructing facilities to do that. Standard Oil Company (New Jersey), for instance, is spending $200 million to build two desulfurization plants. But reducing sulfur in oil to, say, 0.5 percent adds substantially to the cost.

Changing SO_2 Into Something Else

The most effective and potentially least expensive method of controlling SO_2 is chemical removal from flue gas. A number of methods are under development, and one has been tried out commercially. This first commercial installation to control SO_2, put in by Combustion Engineering Inc. at a Union Electric plant in St. Louis, is a "throwaway" system, meaning that it yields no usable byproducts. It cost about $1.4 million to install and Combustion Engineering estimated operating costs at 37 cents per ton of coal. But Union Electric reports it found the operating costs to be around 80 cents to $1 a ton. The utility, moreover, has been experiencing technical difficulties with the system. But when it works, it is effective, removing 85 percent or more of the sulfur dioxide when firing coal containing 3.4 percent sulfur. It does this by feeding pulverized limestone into the furnace and wet-scrubbing the gas as it leaves the air heater. The process yields large quantities of waste materials, notably calcium sulfate and sulfite, products of chemical reactions between the limestone and sulfur oxides. This method appears feasible for companies under pressure to do something about their SO_2 emissions right away, but in the long run it could contribute to water and land pollution unless the waste materials are carefully disposed of.

In Monsanto's catalytic oxidation (Cat-Ox) process, sulfur dioxide is converted into sulfur trioxide, which turns into sulfuric acid mist as it combines with water vapor in the stack gas. The acid is then trapped and removed. The Monsanto process yields 78 percent sulfuric acid, which is too dilute for many industrial uses and is difficult to ship very far because of its corrosive nature.

Monsanto is now installing its first commercial-size demonstration plant at an Illinois Power installation at Wood River, Illinois. The National Air Pollution Control Administration will pay more than half the construction cost of the $6.8 million plant. Another sort of subsidy will be supplied to Illinois Power by Monsanto itself. Its contract makes Monsanto responsible for disposing of the sulfuric acid for five years after completion of the SO_2 removal system. The exact costs of the overall system aren't known, but Illinois Power officials think it will be cheaper than buying low-sulfur coal.

Still another large-scale test of SO_2 removal is scheduled at a 150,000-kilowatt Boston Edison Company plant. The technique, based on removing SO_2 with magnesium oxide, was developed by Chemical Construction Corporation, a subsidiary of Boise Cascade Corporation, and by the Basic Chemicals division of Basic Inc. Economic operation requires regeneration and reuse of the magnesium oxide, and this has not yet been proved out on a large scale.

Probably the most promising technique of SO_2 removal to appear so far has been developed jointly by Ionics Inc. and Stone & Webster Engineering Corporation. It is based on chemical scrubbing of the SO_2 with sodium hydroxide, all of which is regenerated. The technique, tried out at a pilot plant in Tampa, Florida, scrubs about 95 percent of the SO_2, which is converted into highly concentrated and salable sulfuric acid. The two companies claim that at the present price of sulfur their process could yield a net operating profit for a utility. Specifically, they estimate that its operation at a 1,200-megawatt power station in the Midwest, burning coal with 3.5 percent sulfur, would yield a 7 percent return after Federal income taxes, the same profit as on electric power. These calculations assume the sale of 340 thousand tons of 99 percent sulfuric acid a year at $18.50 a ton. Large-scale reclaiming of sulfur compounds from stack gas, of course might upset the economics of sulfur.

Most of these SO_2 removal methods are believed also to scrub some of the oxides of nitrogen. There is nothing very promising on the horizon yet to remove most nitrogen oxides economically. Modifications of the combustion process, catalytic reduction, caustic scrubbing, and other techniques are being studied, but none has even reached a pilot-plant stage.

Into the Ocean One Way or Another

In the control of water pollution, the great problem is not so much a lack of new methods as an excessive adherence to the old. Even though the Federal Government expects to spend more than $2 billion in this area in the current fiscal year, it does little to encourage long-range thinking and planning. The Federal funds go overwhelmingly into construction of old-fashioned sewage-treatment plants, which are not designed to cope with today's complex chemical pollutants.

A particularly eloquent critic of Federal programs to control water pollution is Dr. Harvey Ludwig, president of Engineering-Science, Inc., an affiliate of Zurn Industries, Inc. Instead of pouring billions into outdated bricks and mortar, says Ludwig, the Government should raise its expenditure on regional studies about twentyfold and greatly expand its meager research budget. Present Federal spending on regional studies amounts to $8 million a year; a full study of a single major body of water such as Chesapeake Bay or Lake Erie might cost as much as $20 million.

As part of his regional approach, Ludwig suggests that individual communities combine forces to build big sewage-treatment plants capable of handling waste from a large area. If these plants could be located near a seacoast, pipelines would be constructed to bypass the estuaries, the spawning areas for much marine life, and discharge the treated effluent far out at sea. Under present methods of disposal, sewage is often deposited in the estuaries, ruining them, and then it flows into the ocean. As Ludwig puts it, "God is taking it into the ocean without a pipeline." For inland cities, Ludwig proposes regional plants to treat sewage so thoroughly that a minimum amount of harmful substances would be released into waterways. Eventually, he suggests, the answer is indefinite recycling and reuse of water, because even the most stringent treatment would still permit unwanted nutrients and toxins to flow into the streams and lakes. Says Ludwig: "We should leave the streams alone."

There is need for great improvement in the waste-treatment plants now being built. "The old plants," says Ludwig, "were built like parks and monuments—to last a million years." There is no reason for them to stretch as they do over acres and acres of valuable land. Ludwig would like to see sewage plants become as compact as a small oil refinery—and he would put them underground. "You could put one under Grand Central Station and no one would know it."

Ludwig's concept of underground sewage plants rests on the development of a highly compact, drum-shaped, rotating filter that would make it possible to substitute mechanical filtration for the gravitational settling that now takes place slowly in big tanks. The size of these settling tanks is what makes conventional treatment plants so huge and, in terms of land use, so expensive. With mechanical filtration, the plants could be reduced to one third, perhaps even one fifth, of their present size.

The filter could probably be developed for about $1 million, Ludwig says. But neither Engineering-Science nor Zurn Industries can afford that big a speculative expenditure, and

Ludwig (like others in the pollution-control field) does not want to accept a Federal subsidy for the research, because the company would lose proprietary rights to the device if it were developed with Federal aid. "The Federal position encourages a company like ours to keep on designing big fat sewers going downhill," complains Dr. Ludwig. "How is that ever going to clean up the environment?"

Future treatment plants are likely to discard the largely inefficient settling tanks used in primary treatment, which removes some of the gross solids, and go directly to secondary processing. This stage, in the conventional method, relies on aeration of the sludge and digestion of organic matter in it by bacteria. But in this chemical age that kind of treatment isn't quite good enough. Persistent pesticides and herbicides, salts, and certain acids and dyes pass right through secondary treatment, largely unaffected. And the bacteria are sometimes incapacitated by acids and other potent industrial chemicals in the sewage.

Researchers in demonstration plants have sought to remove such undesirable nutrients and toxins by means of tertiary treatment. This takes the effluent through chemical treatment and, frequently, filtering columns of activated carbon. In a few demonstration plants the use of bacteria has been discarded completely in favor of chemical treatment. Advanced treatment can produce water good enough or nearly good enough to drink, as has been shown at a full-scale operating plant on the California side of Lake Tahoe, and at small demonstration plants at Salt Lake City, Rocky River, Ohio, and elsewhere. (See "The Limited War on Water Pollution," *Fortune*, February [1970].) These plants turn sewage into a resource: water that can be used for irrigation, for recreation ponds, for cooling at electric-power plants.

Biological processing is generally a lot cheaper than chemical, and municipalities with few industries using their sewers are likely to continue to rely on bacteria. Heavily industrialized cities, on the other hand, may switch to chemical treatment. The largest chemical pilot plant so far has been designed by Engineering-Science for Cleveland. If this approach works out, Cleveland may treat most of its sewage chemically, becoming the first large US city to do so.

The Mercury Hazard

Treatment of industrial wastes rests on a more solid technological base because it is often tied to process control. Furthermore, the continuing entry of big corporations into industrial-pollution control makes the situation more hopeful than on the municipal front. Already operating in pollution control are such companies as Monsanto, Dow Chemical, Du Pont, Westinghouse, and even Coca-Cola (through its recent acquisition of Aqua-Chem). Johns-Manville, one of the latest entrants, . . . [in July 1970] established a division to coordinate and greatly expand the company's pollution-control activities. To start with, Johns-Manville scientists are analyzing manufacturing processes with the idea of controlling wastes at the source.

Stopping industrial wastes at the source would be economically advantageous—some materials might be recovered and reused—and beneficial from the standpoint of public health as well. To take one example, indiscriminate discharge of compounds of mercury, used in production of caustic soda and chlorine and in other processes, has created a public health hazard that is only now being recognized in the United States and Canada. Anaerobes (microorganisms that live without free oxygen) break the compounds down into poisonous methyl mercury, which passes from organism to organism through food chains to fish and man. In Japan, episodes of poisoning from eating fish that contained mercury go back as far as the early 1950s; more than one hundred people have died or become seriously ill. Just this year [1970] US and Canadian scientists began to detect high mercury concentrations in fish taken from various lakes and streams.

Mercury is only one of many kinds of harmful substances that man is discharging into the environment, and to cope with their combined and cumulative effects will take much more than just tinkering, even expensive tinkering. Above all, it will take a lot of thought. Efforts to remedy environmental ills are often lacking in imagination and perspective. It is not enough to deal with this or that pollution problem on a piecemeal, short-run basis. We must consider the complex interaction of a myriad of pollutants and their long-run impact on the web of life, and undertake coordinated, systematic remedies. Unless we think more about the future, the future will turn out to be more polluted than the present.

THE NEED FOR INTERNATIONAL COOPERATION [3]

US health inspectors turned up their noses recently and sent a shipment of Italian cheeses back to Italy when a sample revealed traces of a toxic substance. The Italians, examining the cheese under their own microscopes, quickly discovered that the offending substance was US-made pesticide, which had been sprayed on Italian pastures.

The episode, related by Dr. Hilliard Roderick, environmental director of the twenty-two-nation Organization for Economic Cooperation and Development [OECD], is more than ironic. If the United States tightened its health regulations on pesticide contamination in imported foods and the Italians clamped down on American pesticides, two new obstacles to international trade would be created.

Two further obstacles could arise from the concern over noise pollution and other potential damage to the environment from the supersonic transport. There is some chance that such objections will help shoot down the US supersonic transport project. [SST plans were rejected in 1971.—Ed.] Tough US curbs on noise and jet pollution also could bar the Anglo-French Concorde from the United States, thus killing its chances of commercial success. If this happens, the

[3] From "Trade Collides With Ecology." *Business Week*. p 72-3+. Ja. 23, '71. Reprinted from the January 23, 1971, issue of *Business Week* by special permission. Copyrighted © 1971 by McGraw-Hill, Inc.

French government has privately warned the United States that it could retaliate against US jumbo jets.

Hundreds of such cases are likely to spring up as nations toughen their controls to protect the environment. At a three-day conference in Washington . . . [in January 1971], sponsored by the Atlantic Council and the Battelle Memorial Institute, corporate executives and environment officials from the United States, Europe, and Japan voiced fears that a whole new array of nontariff barriers to international trade and investment may result. Some American businessmen also worry that US companies will be at a disadvantage in world competition if the United States moves further and faster than other countries in imposing costly antipollution regulations on private industry.

Ian MacGregor, chairman of American Metals Climax, Inc., put it this way: "We all favor the objective of a cleaner environment. But the problem is that the rest of the world is lagging behind the United States in pollution control and I fear the added financial burden to American industry could weaken our competitiveness in world trade."

Businessmen are worried about other potential problems that environmental controls could create in international operations:

> If major trading nations get too far out of step in regulations that affect the design of products and equipment, the result could be to fragment world markets. For example, autos that meet exhaust rules in some countries might be barred from others.
>
> Environmental controls affect international investment patterns, by making it costlier to build and operate plants in one country than in another. The French chemical company, Progil, for instance, canceled plans for a plant near Amsterdam in the face of local protests against pollution and shifted its project to Antwerp last fall.

American companies fear that other governments will pick up more of the cost of cleaning up industrial pollution, thus putting US concerns at a competitive disadvantage.

Engineering a "Trade-Off"

One answer to such problems is for industrial nations to coordinate their policies on protecting the environment in order to avoid distortions of world markets. Said Henry Fowler, former United States Treasury Secretary and now a partner in the New York investment firm of Goldman, Sachs & Company: "It is crucially important to achieve a commonality of approach to minimize the side effects of pollution control on international trade and investment."

For that purpose, the meeting called for creation of an international ecological institute financed by governments to try to harmonize environmental standards among nations. Actually, a number of such efforts are already under way. The OECD recently set up a committee on environment in Paris. It is attempting to create an "early warning system" to advise members in advance of actions in such fields as environment and health regulations that could have international repercussions.

The rash of uncoordinated actions against cyclamates is an example of the kind of confusion the committee will try to avoid. The sudden US ban late in 1969 touched off disparate rulings by other countries and created uncertainties over the use of cyclamates from Switzerland to Mexico.

Assistant Secretary of State Christian Herter, Jr., who heads the department's newly created Office of Environmental Affairs, told the committee at its initial meeting last November [1970] that the unilateral US ban on cyclamates was a "mistake," and that the United States "should have let our allies know what was being done."

Initial studies by the committee are aimed at suggesting guidelines for member countries on controlling pollution from automobiles, power plants, and pulp and paper mills.

It also plans to call a conference on pesticides. The committee seeks to balance the requirements of economic growth against the need for protecting the environment. "The essence of the problem is the trade-off," Herter emphasized.

Meanwhile, the United Nation's Economic Commission for Europe, which includes Communist countries as well as Western nations, has scheduled a conference in Prague next May [1971] to lay the groundwork for coordinating environmental policies of member governments. The staff of the General Agreement on Tariffs & Trade, in Geneva, is trying to unravel the tangle of nontariff barriers posed by pollution, safety, and health controls. In 1972, a mammoth 120-nation UN Conference on the Human Environment in Stockholm will try to set global guidelines for coping with environmental pollution and managing natural resources. [See Section V, Editor's Introduction; "American World Policy," by Russell E. Train; and "New Journey of Hope," by Maurice F. Strong, below.—Ed.]

But the obstacles to international coordination of environmental policies are formidable. Robert Toulemon, the Common Market Commission's director for industrial affairs, warned the Washington conference that Europe and the United States are likely to remain out of step on environmental controls for some time. He argued that the Common Market still lags behind the United States economically and cannot afford to spend as much on cleaning up pollution. And the six member-countries are just beginning to formulate common strategies for dealing with environmental problems. Developing countries, for their part, are reluctant to divert scarce resources to pollution control. A retired Brazilian army general, who is a director of several companies, says: "We must be careful not to hold down economic development for the sake of fighting a shadow."

Divergent Standards

Such divergent objectives have created a jungle of environmental standards that companies must deal with in worldwide operations. The Common Market, for example, recently adopted standards for car exhausts, but left member governments the choice of maintaining separate national standards for cars sold in the domestic market. Auto makers will have to meet the Common Market criteria for cars exported to other member countries, but may build cars to national specifications for home use. Other European countries have different standards. Says a Ford spokesman in Brussels: "For Ford in Europe, the effect of not having a single standard on emission control increases the number of engine types manufactured seven-fold."

On the US West Coast, a spokesman for Kaiser Steel Corporation says: "There can be no doubt that Kaiser Steel is placed at a competitive disadvantage by complying with pollution controls that are stricter than those that are applicable to our foreign competitors. Based on the growing opposition of environmentalists, there is some question whether new steel-producing furnaces will be permitted in the West in the future." This opposition is one of the factors that has led Kaiser to explore the possibility of a huge joint steel-making venture with Armco Steel Corporation and British Steel Corporation in Australia. Kaiser stresses that an Australian mill would have to have the latest pollution abatement equipment, but at least it could be built.

Despite the differences in national standards, there is no escape from mounting public demands in all industrial countries for stricter protection of the environment—often echoing the furor over pollution in the United States. Says an official of an international oil company: "Companies are just buying time when they seek out areas where pollution is not at stake. Sooner or later, they will have to face up to controls."

In fact, it is debatable whether US pollution curbs are any stricter than in many European countries. John R.

Wheaton, director of Du Pont de Nemours (Deutschland), thinks that German pollution laws, for example, may be tougher than in the United States. Germany "has moved forward faster in this direction than many parts of the United States," he says. Sweden and the Netherlands are certainly stricter. Japan, with some of the world's worst pollution problems, has lagged in measures to protect the environment, but is catching up fast.

For US companies that make pollution control equipment, the rising environmental concern is creating bigger markets abroad as well as at home. The Commerce department estimates that the Common Market countries and Switzerland will spend about $375 million a year in the early 1970s for antipollution equipment.

Westinghouse Electric Corporation is one US company that is selling to that market and others overseas, through licensees and subsidiaries as well as exports from the United States. Kurt Katz, general manager of Westinghouse's water quality control division, finds that the problems of differing regulations overseas are no greater than among states and municipalities in the United States. "Waste treatment unit operations are systems," Katz says. "We try to optimize that system to perform the function our customer is interested in."

Meantime, US managers are learning to cope with public outcries against industrial pollution all over the world. When Du Pont opened its fibers plant at Uentrop, Germany, local fishermen became alarmed about the plant's discharge into the Lippe river, even though the effluent is purified by a biological system. To calm them, Wheaton called in the press, fishing club members, and local officials, and demonstrated the purity of the effluent by drinking a tumblerful. The complaints died down. "Strangely enough," Wheaton says, "the fish now congregate at our discharge point. They seem to like what's coming out."

THE MOVEMENT: PUBLIC SUPPORT FALTERS [4]

Activist environmental organizations have fallen into the doldrums this winter. Contributions and membership levels have not increased at rates anticipated a year ago, and "ecology" seems to have lost some of its charisma.

Some observers are speaking ominously of an environmental backlash created by fears that the costs of environmental reform are more than the public is willing to pay. It would probably be more nearly accurate to say that there has been a subsiding of the wave of public enthusiasm for the cause which swelled around the time of Earth Day on 22 April 1970.

The old-line, nonpolitical conservation groups, many of which have a solid base of support from foundations, have not reported much suffering. The Izaak Walton League, the Conservation Foundation, and the Wildlife Federation, for example, report that 1971 was a year of steady, if not exciting, increase in membership.

But the activist organizations, most of them new, which rely on continuous publicity and public enthusiasm, are feeling the pinch. Gifts to them are not tax deductible and foundations are legally prohibited from supporting lobby groups. The Sierra Club must be included among these, because in 1969 it lost the security of its tax-deductible status after it began overt lobbying activities. For the Sierra Club, "The problem came up overnight. In September everything was rosy," says Richard Lahn of the Washington office. At a November board meeting, the club laid on a staff-hiring freeze and put restrictions on travel, telephone, and postage spending. In a staff memorandum it was explained that new monthly memberships were substantially less than the projected three thousand, that book sales had dropped sharply, and that overdue bills were piling up. Some think . . . [the

[4] From "Environmental Action Organizations Are Suffering from Money shortages, Slump in Public Commitment," by Constance Holden, a staff editor. *Science.* 175:394-5. Ja. 28, '72. Copyright 1972 by the American Association for the Advancement of Science. Reprinted by permission.

1971] hike in membership dues—from $12 to $15—has contributed to the financial slowdown. Sierra Club publications are not selling as well as expected, partly because of the high cost of the coffee-table variety and also because Time-Life is making inroads on the market with a series of luxurious books on natural wonders.

Friends of the Earth (FOE), a lobby group established in July 1969 by former Sierra Club executive director David Brower, is in more serious straits. Its membership, now 22,000, has not risen significantly in the last six months. The organization is now $250,000 in the red because it hasn't been able to summon the money to pay back substantial loans it procured in order to get launched. Drastic trimming has resulted—the San Francisco office has been closed down, and offices in New York and Albuquerque are folding. An expensive direct-mail campaign conducted . . . [in 1971] turned out to be a losing gamble.

Entering Phase II

Environmental Action, the group that spent three months and $100,000 organizing the 1970 Earth Day, is now running on the thinnest shoestring of all. The staff of nine are working on subsistence wages of $55 a week. Direct-mail solicitations have produced a disappointing yield. "So much of the energy that should be going into action programs is going into worrying about the money situation," laments the group's coordinator Sam Love. But, "we're not going to fold —because we're stubborn."

The money slump has also affected Zero Population Growth (ZPG), the only population control organization that has forsworn deductibility for political activity. ZPG's Washington-based director of political activities Carl Pope says ZPG's problems are somewhat different from those of other environmental groups because of the diffuse and long-term nature of the problem. People might be more concerned "if the earth were being worn away by all of our footsteps," he says, but well-publicized developments (such as, hopefully, the forthcoming report by the President's Commission on Population Growth and the American Future) are needed to keep people worried. The movement was not helped when the press made front-page stories of a report sponsored by the Washington Center for Metropolitan Studies which purported to show that the baby boom had been supplanted by a "baby bust." But the real blow in ZPG's solar plexus has been delivered by Right to Life citizens' groups who have mobilized vocal antiabortion campaigns. While ZPG's emphasis is on family planning rather than abortion, the Right to Life people "stopped us in our tracks," says Pope. The ZPG's immediate goal, which is to push through Congress a joint resolution endorsing a national policy of population stabilization, is now in cold storage.

Discussions with the groups mentioned above confirm one FOE staff member's observation that "the road for nondeductible groups is a very hairy road indeed."

None of the reasons for the leveling off of public enthusiasm are particularly obscure. The campuses are not presently a prime source of emotional energy. The Nixon economic freeze has made nondeductible charitable donations an early casualty, and many political donations are now going to presidential candidates rather than to causes. Some people feel, too, that the market has become glutted with public-interest lobby groups that the public, now back in its normal state of anxious apathy, is reluctant to support.

In a way, environmental activism has entered its own Phase II. Now that the consciousness-raising stage is over and pollution is firmly associated with evil, few issues are susceptible to black and white interpretations. Battles are moving off the front page and into the back rooms of the legislatures and the courts. The Environmental Defense Fund (EDF) and the National Resources Defense Council, for example, both of which are involved in environmental court battles, are still reasonably well off. Rod Cameron of the four-year-old EDF points out that EDF is engaged in specific, visible activities and thus is more assured of a stable financial constituency.

Assurance that the issue is still foremost in the concerns of Americans comes from a poll conducted last summer [1971] by Common Cause, the national citizens' lobby. The 35,000 persons who answered the fourteen-item questionnaire ranked environmental protection as second in importance only to withdrawal from Vietnam.

Nevertheless, the activist groups are realizing that better planning and increased expertise will be necessary to press their cause within government. Local citizens' groups are increasingly addressing themselves to such specific projects as trash recycling or attempts to block inner-city expressways and undesirable power plants. But in Washington, the activist groups, many of which are manned by young people barely out of college, must work their way behind the scenes and into the tough legal and technical complexities that surround policy making.

The backlash they face comes not from the public, but from businesses and industries that are finally taking the movement seriously and are responding forcefully—with stepped-up lobbying; sophisticated advertising campaigns proclaiming their dedication to sunshine and green grass; and employee "education" programs, which, crudely summed up, sometimes amount to saying: "Which do you want, clean air or a job?" (an approach commonly called environmental blackmail).

Environmental activism has lost a lot of innocence since the flowery euphoria that characterized Earth Day. Typically, the young people working in the little offices in Washington still believe they have the public behind them and are determined to stick with their increasingly difficult cause. No one is particularly concerned that ecology might be a passing fad, because, as they say, "If it's a fad, it's the last fad."

V. THE WAY AHEAD: SOME PROFFERED SOLUTIONS

EDITOR'S INTRODUCTION

The United Nations Conference on the Human Environment, held in Stockholm June 5-16, 1972, appears to have given new life to what may have been a flagging cause and has certainly restored our confidence in the old cliché, "Where there's a will, there's a way." Although most press accounts reported that the conference was only moderately successful, we know at least that people everywhere are aware of the problems facing them, that they are putting their minds to work on those problems, and that a spirit of cooperation animates their work.

The basic purpose of this section is to demonstrate precisely how far our political leadership has come (and the public, too) in an appreciation of the ecological troubles afflicting mankind. Some of us may be surprised by the speed and energy with which our officials have seriously studied and acted upon the issues. Others may despair that their efforts are far too meager to date, given the scope and urgency of the challenge. Whatever the case, it is reassuring to know that some action is being taken.

The first article in this section sets forth the environmental views of Senator George S. McGovern of South Dakota, the Democratic candidate for the presidency in 1972. The next article is given over to a summary of the views of the Nixon Administration on the subject, specifically as presented by the chairman of the President's Council on Environmental Quality, Russell E. Train. In the third article, a correspondent for *The Christian Science Monitor* explains the potential—and the pitfalls—inherent in the recently negotiated US-Soviet environmental agreement. Whatever its shortcomings, the agreement comes as an encouraging sign that environmental issues have at last been recognized as important—too important to be subject to ideological maneuvering by either side.

The fourth article in this section, taken from *Forbes* magazine, strikes a less happy but equally important note in describing the efforts underway in various states and localities to transfer environmental blight to other communities —or at least bar it by erecting "Keep Out" signs directed at people as well as industry. We are again reminded that the days of the booster and of facile Chamber of Commerce enthusiasm may indeed be numbered. The fifth article is devoted to a heartening account of what individuals around the country can do and have been doing to get positive action on the quality of the environment in their own communities. And in the last contribution, the secretary general of the Stockholm conference, Maurice F. Strong, the Canadian diplomat who is an Under-Secretary-General of the UN, announces the start of a "new journey of hope" for mankind. The way will be long and difficult, he warns, but at last a start has been made.

ACTION PLAN FOR THE FEDERAL GOVERNMENT [1]

Pollution of our environment is increasing alarmingly. It is already so extensive that the Federal Government must play a major role in confronting this national problem. The Government can act in a positive way to stop pollution, but there is no doubt that it will have to envisage penalties for those who fail to do their share.

The problem the nation faces is almost overwhelming. Among the major areas for action are clean water, clean air and solid waste disposal.

Water is essential for life, but by the end of the century it may be in short supply. We will not be able to waste it;

[1] Article, "The Federal Government and the Environment," by George S. McGovern, United States Senator from South Dakota. *Current History.* 59:82-3+. Ag. '70. Reprinted by permission of Current History, Inc.

water will have to be reused many times. Yet we continue to dispose of waste in our rivers and lakes, and even pesticides, which are essential to farming, eventually seep into the water.

More than 142 million tons of pollutants are released into the air over the United States every year—three quarters of a ton for every man, woman and child. Virtually all air pollution results from some kind of combustion or burning —gasoline in automobile engines, coal, oil or other fuels in industrial plants, generators and heating plants, or the incineration of garbage or other refuse.

Solid waste is piling up as we use more disposable containers. It is increasing by more than 4 percent annually; every day United States municipal and private collection services pick up the equivalent of more than five pounds of trash and garbage for every American.

Congress has created a positive legislative framework for improving our environment. Among the most important laws adopted in recent years are: The Water Resources Act of 1964, the Water Resources Planning Act of 1965, the Highway Beautification Act of 1965, the Clean Air Act of 1965, the Air Quality Act of 1967, the Clean Water Restoration Act of 1966, the Solid Wastes Act of 1965 and the National Environmental Policy Act of 1969.

Now life must be breathed into the law by the appropriation of adequate funds. Governments, at all levels, will have to spend as much as $150 billion in the next fifteen to twenty years to clean up pollution. Industry will have to spend the same amount. But in the 1969 fiscal year, the Federal Government is spending only $3.7 billion or only 1.8 percent of the total budget on the environment.

The Administration has now proposed a program to improve the nation's environment. Uniform standards would be set for water purity and municipalities would be encouraged by $4 billion in Federal grants to build sewage treatment plants. Research would be conducted on a "virtually pollution-free" car. Cash incentives would be paid for hauling old cars to junkyards. An effort would be made to open new recreation areas.

While this is a useful program, it must be linked with a far greater program for stopping pollution. If adequate financing is forthcoming, each problem can be brought under strong attack.

Stiffer Penalties Required

The Federal Government could encourage local governments to stop disposal of human and industrial wastes in the water. Safeguards would be ready for policing the water once it is clean and for preventing new industrial and housing developments from becoming polluters. Good soil conservation techniques would help stop run-off of water containing pesticides. But this positive program, which is within our reach, must be accompanied by stiffer penalties against industrial and municipal discharge into lakes and rivers. Both Federal and state agencies will have to be prepared to levy stiff penalties if necessary. Fines of up to $10 thousand a day would be authorized by the [Nixon] Administration's proposal.

Congress has adopted a program aimed at establishing five-year air-quality improvement programs in fifty-seven "air-quality control regions." The setting of Federal standards would provide a basis for stronger enforcement of clean air rules; penalties could go as high as $10 thousand a day.

Naturally, we must ensure that solid wastes do not become an increasing blight. But even if this form of pollution is kept within bounds, we still will face the problem of disposing of it. Over $800 million has already been appropriated for research and action on waste disposal. Now increased attention should be given to reusing solid wastes. More than $1 billion worth of metal can be salvaged each year. Recycled waste paper can help preserve our forests from accelerated depletion.

In all of these fields, the actions of the Federal Government can and should be positive. It should be able to devise and implement effective programs to stop the progressive despoilment of the environment and then to improve substantially the air, land, and water.

But recent events, such as the disastrous oil spills on our shores, show that the Federal Government must also be armed with effective punitive weapons. While positive action will, we hope, eventually bring an end to pollution, polluters will, in the meantime, have to be discouraged from continued practices. The economic cost of polluting can be made as high as the profit accrued from pursuing policies which show little regard for the preservation of the environment. Economic penalties can serve this purpose, although they are far less desirable than voluntary, constructive action by government and industry.

Government and industry cannot end pollution themselves. Each individual has an obligation to himself and his neighbors to work toward the improvement of the environment. The Federal Government can help individuals to do their job.

The McGovern-Hart Bill

Senator Philip Hart (Democrat, Michigan) and I have proposed the Environmental Protection Act of 1970 which would serve just this purpose. It would provide that:

> The Congress finds and declares that each person is entitled by right to the protection, preservation, and enhancement of the air, water, land, and public trust of the United States and that each person has the responsibility to contribute to the enhancement thereof.

The act would authorize any person to bring suit in Federal court against any person or organization which is causing pollution. The court would be empowered to order action to be taken that would end the offending pollution, once the plaintiff proved his case. [In authorizing citizen suits to protect the environment, the McGovern-Hart bill goes beyond anything thus far proposed by the Nixon Administration.—Ed.]

The most important feature of this act would be the strengthening of the right of individuals to use the Federal Government's judicial system to protect their own environment. Because the environment concerns every person, it is fitting that every person be given the right to protect it. At the same time, of course, each individual should act to preserve it.

AMERICAN WORLD POLICY [2]

From the beginning of his Administration, President Nixon has given high priority to environmental protection as a matter of both domestic and international policy. As he stated, we must act as one world to protect the human environment. This [United Nations] conference [on the Human Environment] provides a unique opportunity for such a united effort.

An immense diversity of nations is gathered here from every region of the earth. We are brought together by a common concern for the quality of human life, the everyday life of people throughout the world. Our subject is much broader than pollution. It includes the kind of communities in which people live. It includes the way resources will be managed for billions of people today and still more billions in the future. Our concern is that all nations of the world should better understand and better control the interaction of man with his environment and that all peoples, now and in future times, should thereby achieve a better life.

In addressing this universal subject of the human environment, every nation's view is conditioned by its own historical experience.

[2] From Statement by Russell E. Train, chairman of the President's Council on Environmental Quality, before the United Nations Conference on the Human Environment, Stockholm, Sweden, June 6, 1972. *Department of State Bulletin.* 67:106-12. Jl. 24, '72.

When my country was very young and President Thomas Jefferson resided at the edge of the Virginia wilderness at Monticello, what distinguished our new republic was not wealth or industry, in which we were not at all impressive, but the compelling force of an idea newly put into practice. This idea was that a nation of immigrants, equal under the law and exercising their right to "the pursuit of happiness," could settle and cultivate a continental wilderness and establish in it their free institutions. For a century and more, we were largely preoccupied with that undertaking.

Some sixty-five years ago, when the American frontier was a thing of the past, President Theodore Roosevelt wrote with admiration about this continental adventure—but he struck a new and more ominous note. Our natural resources, he said, were being rapidly depleted; and he continued with these words:

> The time has come to inquire seriously what will happen when our forests are gone, when the coal, the iron, the oil, and the gas are exhausted, when the soils shall have been still further impoverished and washed into the streams, polluting the rivers, denuding the fields, and obstructing navigation. These questions do not relate only to the next century or to the next generation. It is time for us now as a nation to exercise the same reasonable foresight in dealing with our great natural resources that would be shown by any prudent man in conserving and wisely using the property which contains the assurance of well-being for himself and his children.

Unfortunately, our country did not always follow that good advice. Particularly in the generation just past, we not only committed many of the faults Theodore Roosevelt criticized; we went further and, through inadequate control of our increasingly powerful technology, imposed burdens on our environment, urban and rural alike, such as he never dreamed of.

Policy of the United States

Now the United States is altering its course. We have examined the costs of correcting the most obvious of these problems—pollution—and we have begun to pay the high price of corrective action too long delayed.

Of course, the environmental afflictions we are coping with are largely those of an affluent nation. My country enjoys economic blessings such as many another country earnestly desires to achieve. The United States Government remains convinced that other nations throughout the world can and must increasingly enjoy the same blessings of economic growth and overcome the curse of poverty. In this Second Development Decade [the 1970s, for the UN Development Program] it remains the firm purpose of the United States to assist in that global effort through the United Nations and otherwise.

My country has learned that economic development at the expense of the environment imposes heavy costs in health and in the quality of life generally—costs that can be minimized by forethought and planning. We are learning that it is far less costly and more effective to build the necessary environmental quality into new plants and new communities from the outset than it is to rebuild or modify old facilities.

This point bears repetition: The time to do the job of environmental protection is at the outset, not later. It is far cheaper and far easier.

This point holds true for every country at every stage of development. Economic progress does not have to be paid for in the degradation of cities, the ruin of the countryside, and the exhaustion of resources.

And the converse is equally true: Environmental quality and resource conservation for the long future do not have to be paid for in economic stagnation or inequity.

Environmental quality cannot be allowed to become the slogan of the privileged. Our environmental vision must be broad enough and compassionate enough to embrace the full range of conditions that affect the quality of life for all people. How can a man be said to live in harmony with his environment when that man is desperately poor and his environment is a played-out farm? Or when the man is a slum-dweller and his environment is a garbage-strewn street? I reject any understanding of environmental improvement that does not take into account the circumstances of the hungry and the homeless, the jobless and the illiterate, the sick and the poor.

President Nixon, in transmitting to the Congress the first annual report on the quality of our nation's environment, expressed this central thought when he said: "At the heart of this concern for the environment lies our concern for the human condition: for the welfare of man himself, now and in the future."

This insight—the unity of environmental protection and economic well-being—is likely to be one of the most vitally important insights to emerge from this Stockholm Conference. No longer should there be any qualitative difference between the goals of the economist and those of the ecologist. A vital humanism should inspire them both. Both words derive from the same Greek word meaning house. Perhaps it is time for the economist and ecologist to move out of the separate, cramped intellectual quarters they still inhabit and take up residence together in a larger house of ideas, whose name might well be the house of man.

In that larger house, the economist will take full account of what used to be called external diseconomies—such as, pollution and resource depletion—and he will assign meaningful values to the purity of air and water and the simple amenities we once foolishly took for granted. He will develop better measures of true well-being than the conventional gross national product. The ecologist, in turn, will extend his attention beyond the balance of nature to include all those activities of man's mind and hand that make civilized life better than that of the cave dwellers. Both will collaborate to advise the planners and decisionmakers so that cities and countryside of the future will promote the harmonious interaction of man with man and of man with nature, so that resources will remain for future generations, and so that development will lead not just to greater production of goods but also to a higher quality of life.

A Great Beginning

This conference, then, is a great beginning. The many countries here have differing experience and differing priorities, but all of us are reaching toward a new realization of truths taught us by science and by bitter experience. Together we can now broaden our cooperation for the common good—to learn the facts about man's interaction with his earthly environment, to persevere in global development efforts while taking new steps to cleanse and protect the atmosphere, the oceans, the soil, and the forests.

We are, of course, well aware of the limits of international cooperation. It is often fitful and troubled with false starts. The fact of national sovereignty entails frank recognition that many or even most of the crucial environmental actions have to be taken freely by governments and by citizens in their own interest as they see it. In my own country we have taken vigorous measures in recent years to clean up our air and our waters, to reorganize our Government structure for more effective environmental management, and to open up our courts and our processes of government to the invigorating energies of concerned private citizens. In the quest for environmental quality, no need is greater than the development and participation of a concerned, informed, and responsible citizenry.

We in the United States are definitely beginning to make progress in our war on pollution. For example, the level of major air pollutants such as particulates, carbon monoxide, and sulfur oxides has dropped significantly over the past three years in most of our cities. The level of automobile emissions is likewise going down. We still have a long way to go, and there is no room for complacency. But we are demonstrating that the problems of environmental pollution are not insoluble and that they can be dealt with through determined action by government and by citizens.

On the international level, we believe that the United Nations itself has a vital role to play in providing coordination and leadership in the global quest for environmental protection and the quality of life. The Stockholm Conference can help give direction and energy to this historic opportunity for the United Nations.

We have high hopes for the Stockholm Conference. The United States has given its full support to the preparations for it. Of the nearly two hundred recommendations submitted by the Secretariat for our consideration, the great majority have the general or specific support of the United States.

This conference will do more than raise the level of national and international concern for environmental problems; indeed, it has already achieved that. We are confident that it will also generate national, regional, and global action to recognize and solve those problems which have a serious adverse impact on the human environment.

American Proposals at Stockholm

Among the action proposals, in the view of the United States, certain ones stand out as of particular importance:

1. Specifically, the United States supports the establishment of a permanent entity within the United Nations—a twenty-seven-nation Commission of the Economic and Social Council and a high-level Secretariat unit—to coordinate multinational environmental activity and to provide a continuing focus for US attention to environmental problems.

2. The United States supports the creation of a $100 million UN Environmental Fund financed by voluntary contributions from member governments. We are prepared to commit $40 million over a five-year period on a matching basis to the Fund.

3. We support and urge vigorous regional action where this is necessary to adequate management of environmental resources. . . . [In April 1972] the President of the United States and the Prime Minister of Canada signed a pioneering agreement committing both nations to a cooperative long-

term program to protect the water quality of the Great Lakes. But many other major international bodies of water are in similar need. The Baltic, the North Sea, the Mediterranean, the Caspian, the Rhine, the Danube, and many more in every continent cry out for effective regional environmental cooperation. In many of these areas the time for action is rapidly running out.

4. We support efforts to strengthen monitoring and assessment of the global environment and to that end to coordinate and supplement existing systems for monitoring human health, the atmosphere, the oceans, and terrestrial environments.

5. We support coordinated research to strengthen the capability of all nations to develop sound environmental policies and management.

6. We support effective international action to help nations increase their environmental capabilities. This includes the strengthening of training, education, and public information programs in the field of environment, both to develop an environmentally literate citizenry and to train professional environmental scientists and managers. It also includes the establishment of improved mechanisms, such as an international referral system, by which nations can efficiently share their national experience concerning the best methods of solving specific environmental problems in such fields as land-use planning, forest and wildlife management, urban water supply, et cetera.

7. We support creation of a World Heritage Trust to give recognition to the world interest in the preservation of unique natural and cultural sites.

8. We support international agreement at the earliest practicable date to control the dumping of wastes into the oceans, and we also urge appropriate national action to support this objective. The announcement by the delegate of the United Kingdom of the progress recently made toward agreement on an ocean-dumping convention is very welcome, and the United States strongly supports prompt fol-

low-up action. Marine pollution generally should have a high priority for international cooperative action.

I recall last Christmas standing on a magnificent stretch of lonely beach in the Bahamas, watching the great sea waves sweep in from the open Atlantic. Hardly a foot of that beach was without its glob of oil, and the upper reaches of the beach, at the limits of the tide, were littered with the plastic and other nondegradable detritus of our civilization.

9. We support cooperative action to protect genetic resources and to protect wildlife. For example, the United States hopes that this conference will support the objective of a moratorium on the commercial killing of whales. [This objective failed of adoption.—Ed.] Such action would be especially timely in view of the scheduled session of the International Whaling Commission (IWC) in London later this month.

10. Recognizing that uniform pollution standards are not practical or appropriate at this time with respect to pollution which is without significant global impacts, we support the establishment by the appropriate international agencies of criteria upon which national pollution control policies can be based. We believe all nations, in their own interest, will wish to establish and enforce the highest practicable environmental standards needed to protect human health and the environment. Even though these levels will vary among nations, it is important that every effort be made to harmonize differing national environmental policies.

11. We support the identification and evaluation of potential environmental impacts of proposed development activities. Such evaluations should normally lead to higher development benefits in the long term. Likewise, we urge all nations and international organizations to undertake systematic environmental analyses as a normal part of their planning and decision-making activities.

12. Finally, we support the draft Declaration on the Human Environment as a fitting message from this conference

to the world and a further proof of our serious intent. In particular, we support its important provisions concerning the responsibility of states for environmental damage and the obligation of states to supply information on planned activities that might injure the environment of others. We believe that every nation should adopt effective procedures to insure that its neighbors have adequate notice of plans and projects which could significantly affect their environment and that measures should be taken to assure that any such adverse impacts be avoided or minimized.

[For information on how these proposals fared at the conference, see "New Journey of Hope," by Maurice F. Strong, in this section, below.—Ed.]

A Call for Responsibility

The frustration of modern man is twofold. There are those who have not even the basic material equipment for a decent life and who rightfully desire very ardently to acquire it. But there are also those who get much of what they ask for and who for a while go on asking for more—more goods, more services, more electric power, more comfort—until some dark night, alone with themselves, they are moved to ask: Why? What is it all worth if the fields and the forests have been despoiled, the air befouled, the animals reduced, and the broad oceans debased?

The fabric of human happiness is as complex and as delicately balanced as natural processes themselves. Our immense and still-growing power over our surroundings must go together with a new responsibility and a new discipline, the discipline of conserving resources, of limiting our births, of living within the means of the natural support systems on which we depend.

Such thoughts raise difficult questions, and the answers will vary widely from one nation or region to another. But in other respects the environmental and economic problems of this one earth are truly global, and we need to begin systematic analyses of them on a global scale.

Certainly one truth is already undeniable: In our use of resources we must have regard for the needs of those who will come after us. Our most fundamental obligation to future generations is to enhance the estate we transmit to them. Where once man saw himself as custodian of a body of goods and values and traditions, we now realize that he is also custodian of nature itself. Our children will not blame us for what we wisely use, but they will not forgive us for the things we waste that can never be replaced.

Now that the natural order is increasingly subject to human design, our concern, our sense of coresponsibility, must grow commensurately with our new understanding. There is a great excitement in the new journey we are on, a journey of understanding and cooperation, not of mastery and conquest. The essence of twentieth century achievement will lie in our success in the struggle, not with each other or with nature but with ourselves, as we try to adapt creatively to the realization that we are all hostages to each other on a fruitful but fragile planet.

The nations of the earth have many opportunities for working together to meet these challenges. The United States has joined in numerous active bilateral and multilateral arrangements for environmental protection. I have already mentioned the recent Great Lakes Water Quality Agreement with Canada. . . . On May 23 [1972], President Nixon and President Podgorny signed a long-term agreement for close environmental cooperation between the United States and the Soviet Union. [See the following article in this section.] By signing the agreement, both our countries have signaled to the world the priority attention that should be devoted to the environment and to working together on the great causes of peace. Both nations recognize the deep desire of all people to direct their resources to solving the pressing social problems of today.

It will be the task of the United Nations to view all these environmental activities in a global perspective, to speak for the whole world on international environmental questions.

We know the United Nations cannot solve every problem, but it must not set its sights too low. It should be animated by the same essential fact that has brought us together in Stockholm: There is an environmental crisis in this world. The crisis differs, it is true, both in kind and in degree from one nation or region to another, but it is a world crisis nonetheless.

President Nixon, discussing the tasks facing the United Nations in his foreign policy report to the American Congress early this year, described the crisis and the response to it in these words:

> Ours is the age when man has first come to realize that he can in fact destroy his own species. Ours is the age when the problems and complexities of technological revolution have so multiplied that coping with them is, in many ways, clearly beyond the capacities of individual national governments. Ours, therefore must be the age when the international institutions of cooperation are perfected. The basic question is—can man create institutions to save him from the dark forces of his own nature and from the overwhelming consequences of his technological successes?
> I believe profoundly that the answer is yes.

Mr. President and fellow delegates to the Stockholm Conference, it is by our actions, both now and in the years to come, that we have a chance to justify that affirmative answer. We need not act in hysteria, nor credit every prophecy of ecological doom—but act we must. If we act with vision and determination, we will preserve for the children of all nations a chance to live in an earthly home worthy of their needs and hopes.

HANDS ACROSS THE COLD WAR [3]

Pollution is neither capitalist nor Communist. It's both.

That's the tacit admission behind the American-Soviet environmental agreement signed this week in Moscow.

[3] From "Ecology Treaty: Full of Potential," by Peter C. Stuart, staff correspondent. *Christian Science Monitor*. p 1-2. My. 26, '72. Reprinted by permission from *The Christian Science Monitor*. © 1972. The Christian Science Publishing Society. All rights reserved.

"There are . . . market forces at work under both systems which result in maximizing production at the expense of the environment," in the delicate phraseology of President Nixon's top ecological adviser, Russell E. Train, chairman of the Council on Environmental Quality.

So destructive are these "market forces" that they have now prodded the two old ideological enemies into a historic (if cautious) environmental alliance against the common, new foe: pollution.

The document pledges the United States and Soviet Union to "develop cooperation" in eleven pollution problem areas.

Sources close to the negotiations prodding the agreement say the Russians exhibit a sincere environment concern that transcends politics.

For at least two years the Soviet Union has marshaled a comprehensive antipollution program. Water pollution costs the country an estimated $6 billion a year—just about what the United States would spend under pending clean-water legislation.

Another indication of Soviet interest may be the visit here just begun by a top Russian environmental writer to study American antipollution techniques for a forthcoming book.

Despite the blurring of ideological boundaries, however, political philosophy may still confront the new agreement with a major obstacle.

"Urban environment and urban planning" was the first problem-area singled out by chairman Train in which Americans might profit from Soviet experience.

But others question whether much of the heavy-handed planning of the Soviet state-controlled environment might be exportable to America's mixed private-public environment.

The issue of "frivolous consumption"—from luxury electrical appliances to overpackaging—may raise other problems, suggests Joseph Browder, conservation director of the Environmental Policy Center.

Braking the current push for more American-style consumer products in the Soviet government-controlled economy could pose difficult political decisions not required in the American market-controlled economy.

Obstacles to Agreement

Apart from ideology, other hurdles lower the expectations of many environmentalists:

Generality. The joint agreement, befitting its pioneering thrust, turns out to be two and one half pages of mostly generalities. "At the present time we have only defined the general subject matter," Dr. Gordon J. F. MacDonald of the Council on Environmental Quality conceded to newsmen.

"It must somehow get beyond exchanging scientific papers," insists Cynthia Wilson, Washington representative of the National Audubon Society. The President's environmental advisers share her objectives, but cannot guarantee them.

American commitment. The Nixon Administration's record on international pollution makes environmentalists highly skeptical.

The last bilateral environmental agreement—a clean-water pact signed with Canada just six weeks ago—was roundly criticized as a showcase event which committed no additional American money and ducked the phosphate-detergent problem.

In two other areas specifically mentioned for American-Soviet cooperation—supersonic air transports and Arctic petroleum pipelines—the Nixon Administration already has rejected the pleadings of most environmentalists and some affected nations.

The White House opted (unsuccessfully) last year [1971] to underwrite an 1,800 mph SST. Then it approved . . . [in May 1972] an eight-hundred-mile, hot-oil pipeline across Alaska.

The agreement signed . . . in Moscow provides for joint cooperation in areas ranging from legal measures to earthquake predictions. Programs will include exchanges of specialists and information, bilateral meetings, and joint projects.

A Soviet-American supervisory committee . . . will meet only annually, but full-time coordinators will keep the programs moving between sessions. The agreement runs five years, with an automatic five-year extension unless either nation objects.

[On September 21, 1972, Washington and Moscow agreed to undertake 30 joint environmental projects, involving an exchange of up to several hundred scientists and specialists, to protect and improve the environmental quality of cities, farms, rivers, lakes, and the air of both countries. The projects were announced at the conclusion of a three-day meeting of the newly established Joint Committee on Cooperation in the Field of Environmental Protection, and work on some was expected to get under way in November 1972.—Ed.]

TRENDS AT THE STATE AND LOCAL LEVEL [4]

Go West, Young Man. Go to the Big City, Farm Boy. Make It Big. The Fastest-Growing Little Town in Wannabagga County. Growth Is Good. Such for two centuries was the prevailing American ethic: The bigger, the better. The welcome mat was nearly always out, because more people meant more money, more business, more growth. Make our own state (county, town) grow. So welcome. Bring money. Bring markets.

[4] From "Fellow Americans Keep Out!" *Forbes.* 107:22-4+. Je. 15, '71. Reprinted by permission of *Forbes* Magazine.

Oh yes, there were dissenters. Thomas Jefferson believed that industrialization was dangerous to democracy. Henry David Thoreau took to the woods. The Know-Nothing party fought immigration. Cattlemen battled the homesteaders for the West's wide-open spaces. Theodore Roosevelt railed at the greedy interests despoiling the nation. But, prominent as they are in the history books, these men's ideas did not prevail.

The two sides have always existed in this country [says Robert Douglas of the University of Pennsylvania's Regional Science Research Institute]. Those who felt they could make money off economic expansion, and those who felt it was going to ruin an environment they loved. What is changing is that the power in communities is not so centralized as it was in the hands of those who benefit from the growth. The rest of the population is getting more vocal.

As a result, the no-trespassing signs are going up. Though a number of states and localities still assiduously seek new industry, sometimes even they meet new resistance. Many others are becoming choosy, and some are flatly hostile to growth. It's not just: Keep the Smokestacks Out. Welcome, Stranger, the typical American attitude, is fast changing to that of Stranger Get Lost.

Oregon's Governor Tom McCall, a strapping six-foot-six Republican, likes to invite tourists back for another visit but adds: "Just don't come here to live." Delaware Governor Russell W. Peterson, a Republican and former Du Pont executive, has just turned away a $360 million chemical complex from his state. California's Santa Clara County—growth was once its middle name—has dramatically reversed gears. Boulder, Colorado, nervous about losing its small-city convenience and character, is talking about a 100,000 population ceiling. In many rural spots, from the Far West to New England, Boise Cascade and other real estate developers are running into serious roadblocks in plans to build vacation-home communities.

What Price Growth?

Ecology? Pollution? Are these the driving forces behind the new regional exclusionism? In large part, yes. In the last three years, pollution control has become a hot issue nearly everywhere. In the almost forgotten tradition of Jefferson and Thoreau, Americans are asking: What price our growing economy?

But there is more than ecology to these first few signs of regional isolationism. Sociology plays a part. So does anthropology. For example, in his best-selling book, *The Territorial Imperative* (1966), Robert Ardrey wrote:

> If we defend the title to our land . . . we do it for reasons no different, no less innate, no less ineradicable, than do lower animals. The dog barking at you from behind his master's fence acts for a motive indistinguishable from that of his master when the fence was built.

In short, a good many parts of the country are fighting to keep their elbowroom, to defend their turf against growing pressure from the teeming, troubled parts of the country. Don't crowd us, they're saying.

Such a basic human urge may well lie beneath a good deal of the outcry over pollution. It certainly motivates the suburbanite who resists tooth-and-nail the encroachment of urban people and urban problems.

And so people are banding together to fight pollution, to fight industry, to fight more people. Dozens of local groups have sprung up: BAG (Beach Alliance Group) in San Diego County; GASP (Group Against Smelter Pollution) in Phoenix, Arizona; SODA (Stop Ocean Dumping Association) in Wildwood, New Jersey, to mention only a few. Meanwhile, the memberships of national organizations grow to record levels: San Francisco-based Sierra Club—130,000 members; Washington-based Nature Conservancy—26,000 members; New York-based Audubon Society—38,000 members; Zero Population Growth of Los Altos, California—40,000 members; San Francisco-based Friends of the Earth—22,000 members. [For a less optimistic report on these organizations, see

"Environmental Action Organizations Are Suffering from Money Shortages, Slump in Public Commitment," in Section IV, above.—Ed.]

All this happens at a crucial point in US history. For centuries Americans spread out and filled the open spaces. Then, with the agricultural depression of the twenties, Americans began deserting the countryside for the cities. And the population concentrated again. Whereas 49 percent of the population lived in rural areas in 1920, only 37 percent did in 1960. Farm centers in the Midwest became ghost towns. In New England, once-thriving mill towns nearly disappeared.

Now, because of the rising costs and tensions of the overcrowded cities, the United States seems in the early stages of spreading out—again. The urban dweller buying an abandoned farm for weekending is in the vanguard. So is the corporation moving to the suburbs or building a plant in an underdeveloped area; the whole industrial development of the South is part of this phenomenon.

But this new wave of spreading out is in trouble. Today it is nearly impossible to build an electric-power plant, a jet airport, an open-pit mine or a resort community without strong protest from keep-out forces. Even tourism, once considered the ideal "clean" industry, has run afoul of the no-trespassing mood in places.

Certainly, it is commendable that Americans want to protect their families and their communities from pollution; to preserve open spaces; to curb urban sprawl; to count other than economic blessings. The problem is this: Because there is no overall, national plan for use of our resources and land, individual states and counties must struggle alone to protect and improve their quality of life. If they succeed, surely they are going to attract outside industry and people, which may threaten that quality of life. So keep-out policies are formulated. Thus, the country is in danger of becoming compartmentalized, of breaking up into territorial and ecological haves and have-nots.

The New Border Guards

During the Great Depression of the thirties, border guards in California turned away Okies and Arkies, the dispossessed tenant farmers from Oklahoma and Arkansas. The border guards were, in the end, declared unconstitutional. But today, zoning and pollution laws and court decisions do a similar job, on a national and local level, of keeping out people and industries. Legal briefs have replaced border guards.

On the Federal level are the National Environmental Policy Act of 1969, which requires all Federal agencies to consider the environmental effects of their decisions, and the amended Clean Air Act, which gives local air-pollution-control districts great, though as yet untested, power. Also important is the River & Harbor Act of 1899, which lay nearly moribund until resurrected by the Administration in a crackdown on polluters. On state and local levels, tougher pollution and zoning laws are going into effect or being considered. The intent is clear: A pleasant environment is at least as important as industrial expansion. Maybe more so.

The no-trespassing mood is strongest, as might be expected, in the more scenic areas. Take Oregon, again. State Treasurer Robert Straub echoes Governor McCall: "We have a slow rate of growth right now," he says, "and personally I'm very happy with it. I'm not interested in industry for industry's sake, or payroll for payroll's sake, or population just for more population's sake."

A lot of Oregonians agree. The cities of Astoria, Eugene and Portland have recently frozen or restricted various kinds of development. A strong statewide zoning bill is being considered by the Oregon legislature. Straub is pushing for an antipollution tax—"a use fee on air and water," he explains —that would eventually ban pollution-producing companies from the state. And many motorists display a bumper sticker: "Save Oregon for the Oregonians."

In West Virginia, a poor state heavily dependent on coal mining, Governor Arch Moore recently canceled a strip-mining project and warned industry: "We are not going to sell our environment for industrial development." Florida's Governor Reubin Askew takes a similar stand. "We are tightening up our restrictions for commercial development. We want to make sure that we are not simply attempting to grow for growth's sake."

That kind of rethinking is now being done at the county and city levels, too. Look at Santa Clara County, at the southern tip of San Francisco Bay. For years it was one of the country's fastest-growing areas, zooming in population from 290,000 in 1950 to just over a million in 1970.

Now county officials are applying the brakes. "We feel that we should stop, or at least slow down, so we can take care of the major problems we have," says Victor Calvo, chairman of the board of supervisors. Zoning is being tightened up to prevent both high density and sprawl. The county has cut in half its Chamber of Commerce budget and has told the Chamber to spend that money on local studies, not national advertising.

Voters in San Jose, the once expansion-minded county seat, have elected go-slow councilmen. Nearby Palo Alto is considering buying a large area of land rather than permitting it to be developed. Explains Calvo: "They discovered that if they expanded into the foothills, by the time they extended services like roads and schools and police and fire protection, it would actually cost the city money despite the new tax revenue. They would come out ahead if they purchased the land and left it open space."

In Loudon County, Virginia—a state long dominated by pro-expansion interests—county commissioners refused the final permits for a 4,200-home Levittown on 1,200 acres. The Levittown application came just as Boise Cascade was opening the first houses of its Sugarland Run project, which required the usual county services and prompted a reassessment of property in the county. "The property tax bills had

risen for many of our big farm owners," explains County
Planning Director Bruce Drenning, "and they were mad. So
when Levitt came along with a proposal to double the
growth rate without paying its own way in taxes, the commissioners just said no."

Even in Los Angeles County there are signs of change. The
city of Los Angeles, now with 2.8 million people, is considering a new zoning plan that calls for no more than 5 million, vs. the 10 million allowed under the old plan. One
catalyst has been Lesser Los Angeles, founded by Los Angeles
Times columnist Art Seidenbaum in 1969. Seidenbaum feels
the bumper-sticker-and-button outfit influenced the city to
make the population study. "We enabled the Establishment
to understand that there are a lot of people here who do not
favor an enlarged city," he says. Lesser Los Angeles was inspired by Lesser Seattle, a bumper-sticker group formed in
1962, and it in turn inspired several other Lesser groups,
including Lesser San Diego, known by its initials.

Ban the Skyscraper

Perhaps nowhere have the keep-out forces had as much
impact as in San Francisco. A year ago United States Steel
and others were busy planning new skyscrapers there; today,
the United States Steel building, a 550-foot-high, $200 mil-
lion office-hotel complex on the waterfront, has been killed
by the board of supervisors, and an anti-high-rise referendum, which would ban buildings taller than six stories unless
approved by the voters, is scheduled for . . . balloting.

The antiskyscraper forces are led by a businessman and
based on business reasons. "The Establishment says we need
these buildings to bring in money for the city," says Alvin
Duskin, a San Francisco-born dress manufacturer. "But just
what does the city make on high-rise buildings? Nobody has
been able to show me."

Roger Boas, a member of San Francisco's board of supervisors, voted against the United States Steel building because
he thought it should be in the financial district, not on the

waterfront. But he is well aware of the new wave of keep-out sentiment. "Developers have been just too darned greedy in the past, and have neglected aesthetics, air space and the like," he says. "People across the state, across the country, feel they've got to do something to stop this promiscuous growth." Boas himself led the fight against freeways in San Francisco in 1964-65, and since then the construction of freeways there has practically ground to a halt.

In Boulder, Colorado, the no-trespassing signs are going up. "The city is going to examine the whole growth issue," says Community Development Director William Lamont. "Boulder has always had a strong attachment to its natural setting and I think most people, as they come here, say let's shut the door and let nobody else in." One proposal: Rezone the remaining undeveloped industrial land. "If you are going to control growth," explains Lamont, "you should begin by discouraging employment centers rather than housing, which is a by-product."

Listen to David P. Lim, city planning director of Tucson, Arizona's second largest city, with about 260,000 people:

> Since the latter part of last year [1970] . . . there have been more, shall I say, grumblings: "Why do we have to grow? Why do we have this many people?" Tucson was known many years ago as the power structure that didn't want industry, that didn't want this, that didn't want that. Perhaps this feeling is coming back.

There is an economic price in all this, of course. Consolidated Edison Company of New York, for example, has vainly tried to construct a pumped-storage project at Storm King Mountain on the Hudson River fifty miles north of New York City for ten years. A local group, the Scenic Hudson Preservation Conference, has so far blocked the project, is growing in power and expects to win. Meanwhile the metropolitan area faces growing power shortages.

Southern California Edison Company has had similar problems. The people of little Victorville, on the edge of the Mojave Desert ninety miles northeast of Los Angeles, blocked construction of a new coal plant, while to the south, Orange County officials are fighting the expansion of an old gas-oil plant. "It's getting to the point," says Edward A. Hummel, an assistant director of the National Park Service, "where there's just no place the power companies can put up a plant."

In states like Montana and Arizona, the big mining companies are the basis of the economy. In past times, they could do just about anything they wanted. But now the keep-out forces have won some big victories. In Montana, Anaconda's proposed copper-molybdenum open-pit mine at Heddleston was stopped. So was its plan to mine copper at the site of a former chromium mine on government land.

New Montana air-pollution standards could close down Anaconda's Columbia Falls aluminum smelter, which pours fluorides into the air that have caused damage estimated as high as $1 billion to the surrounding forests. "If the state adheres to the law and will give us no variance," says Anaconda Director of Technology George Wunder, "then I presume they will shut the plant down."

Wunder says that if the new pollution standards of Montana and Arizona go into effect, the price of copper, now at 52 cents a pound, will increase by about 6 cents a pound. Already American Smelting & Refining Company has had to cut production in Arizona by 15 percent to meet that state's current standards, and Anaconda is now selling some ore concentrates that went to Arizona to the Japanese instead —at a lower price and hence for a smaller profit.

An $11 Million Loss

Boise Cascade has repeatedly run afoul of the keep-out forces. Its resort projects in California, Nevada, Washington and Connecticut have been harshly criticized by conservation groups and government officials. Unit Six at its Incline Village development at Lake Tahoe, Nevada, was blocked by local authorities, who are considering a ban on all further development there. In New Hampshire, Governor Walter Peterson has warned Boise Cascade that he will closely monitor its project and not allow his state to be plundered by irresponsible out-of-state developers.

Indeed, tougher local building regulations were a big reason Boise Cascade's recreational community subsidiary lost $11 million in 1970, vs. an $11 million profit in 1969.

The fate of Disney's Mineral King ski resort project is now before the Supreme Court. The Cross-Florida Barge Canal, hale and hearty just months ago, has been canceled by President Nixon. The giant jetport under construction next to the Florida Everglades has been canceled. And in New York, the Port Authority, after vainly battling keep-out forces in New Jersey and Long Island for a decade, had to settle for a remote former Air Force base sixty-five miles north of the city as the site of its fourth jetport. But a keep-out movement is building rapidly in nearby Newburgh, even though the new jetport would replace some revenues lost when Stewart Air Force base was closed.

To a large degree, the no-trespassing phenomenon is very much part of the save-the-environment movement. As former Sierra Club President Phillip S. Berry says: "The key issue for conservationists is open space; there can't be any more growth at the expense of our open space or prime scenic areas." Virtually all environmentalists would agree with him, and that's why they are so quick to call for keep-out laws.

Of course, one way of lessening pollution and preserving natural beauty and amenities appears to be through a no-growth economy. Though there is increasing talk about a "steady state" economy, few people take this theory seriously: Population pressures and the demand for higher living standards are irresistible. Moreover, thoughtful environmentalists believe that in order to clean up the environment, more economic growth will be needed. The economists are refining their measurements of growth: A new steel mill is not growth if the pollution it causes equals the value of the steel it produces.

Nonetheless, without subscribing to the no-growth theory, the keep-off-our-turf forces and ecologists are in a stronger position than ever to restrict economic growth. Take, for example, the 1970 amendments to the Clean Air Act. "These amendments give us rather vague but I think wide power in land-use controls and population densities," says Victor Calvo of Santa Clara County, who also is head of the San Francisco Bay Area pollution-control district. "It may very well be that air pollution will be the one criterion that can be readily applied to the problems of land use and density." In other words, an air-pollution control district may be able to simply forbid construction.

Faintly reminiscent of the border guards that kept off the Okies of the thirties is a proposed state plan prepared by California Tomorrow, a respected citizens' group. "Our plan," President Alfred Heller says, "recommends that each state be authorized to establish a capital investment fee of $1,000 that would be charged to each new resident and collected in installments as part of the state income tax process." No-trespassing spelled with dollar signs.

But what about the 60 million to 100 million new Americans expected in the next thirty years? Where are they going to live? Where are they going to work? And play? What about the growing numbers of people taking longer vacations and finding increasing resistance to tourists? Will only the rich be able to afford grass and trees? Will population growth choke instead of fuel economic expansion?

And there is another issue, a very thorny one. It is this: The ecology and no-trespassing movements have a middle-class character. For the poor, the disadvantaged, jobs are still what count. Kentucky's Commissioner of Commerce points out that for a backward state, jobs may be relatively more important than clean air. Interestingly, the battle to keep BASF [Colors and Chemicals, Inc.] out of South Carolina was led by the wealthy citizens of Hilton Head—many of them out-of-staters. Reports . . . indicate that most of the poorer residents favored the plant, pollution or not.

Thought of in this way, no growth or slow growth can take on an anti-Negro, anti-poor character.

Unfortunately, questions like these have been largely avoided by both the Government and the public. It is a situation where typical American individualism and regionalism no longer provide the answers. What is needed is a balanced approach, reconciling the need for economic growth with the equally compelling—but no more so—need for clean air and open spaces. Such planning, to be effective, must be at least statewide—probably nationwide eventually. As things stand, the no-trespassing signs just keep going up and up. And business is increasingly caught in the middle.

WHAT YOU CAN DO [5]

For 130 miles through a rich agricultural and industrial valley in north central Ohio flows the Sandusky River. Its name, of Indian origin, means clear water, but not since the earliest settlers reached Ohio has any man seen the Sandusky run clear.

Ray Grob, owner-operator of a camera shop in Fremont, Ohio, and an avid outdoorsman and Boy Scout leader, was long concerned about the condition of this river that runs through his hometown.

It was not grossly polluted [said Grob], but a lot was needed to clean it up aesthetically and protect it from further damage— from farmland run-off, siltation and industrial waste discharges.

A family canoe trip we took on a scenic river in Michigan in 1964 prompted me to do something about the Sandusky. My two children were small at the time, and I was impressed at how famously we all got along and how well the children did on that trip. I thought it would be a shame if families couldn't always enjoy this kind of experience close to home.

Grob had recently started writing an outdoors column for a local paper in his spare time, and in it he began pro-

[5] Article entitled "What Can You Do to Clean Up the Environment? Plenty!" *Changing Times.* 26:6-11. Mr. '72. Reprinted by permission from *Changing Times*, the Kiplinger Magazine, (March 1972 issue). Copyright 1972 by The Kiplinger Washington Editors, Inc. 1729 H. St. N.W. Washington, D.C. 20006.

moting the idea of declaring the Sandusky a scenic river protected by law from commercial development and pollution. He talked the idea up among his friends. He developed a color slide presentation about the river and showed it to service and civic clubs and government and business officials —to more than one thousand people in all. He produced an illustrated booklet about the scenic and recreational value of the Sandusky. It was a long, slow process of building up interest in communities all along the river valley.

Finally, a friend who shared Grob's concern was elected to the state senate. He introduced a Ray Grob-inspired scenic rivers bill that since has become law. It provided protection for designated rivers and enabled the state to seek Federal funds for easements, parklands and cleanup projects. . . .

People along the Sandusky responded quickly and enthusiastically to the new law. A seventy-mile stretch of the river was declared a scenic area. Last year Fremont developed two new parks on the banks of the river, and the state and other riverside communities put up money for additional parkland and protective easements. Meanwhile, Ray Grob's scout troop "adopted" a one-mile stretch of the river, on which they annually plant hundreds of tree seedlings and conduct litter cleanups. As Grob explained, "We do it to show people that if you concentrate on one thing you can really get something done."

Ray Grob's efforts—and his success—are not unique. Hundreds, perhaps thousands, of concerned citizens like him spend enormous amounts of time and energy on personal projects to protect the environment. Most are committed, persevering individuals of all ages and occupations and interests who believe passionately that people have a right to a clean, livable world. This article tells some of their stories.

"They Even Used Helicopters"

The herd of dwarf Tule elk had long roamed Government-owned land in the Owens Valley of California, on the eastern slope of the Sierras, and the state fish and game commission had regularly permitted numbers of the elk to be slaughtered in order to preserve part of their habitat grasslands for leasing to cattle ranchers.

By 1960 the herd was down to 300 when the commission announced that the year's kill figure would be set at 150. At that point Mrs. Beula Edmiston, a Los Angeles housewife, and fourteen others showed up at a public hearing to protest the commission's order.

We had no organization, but because we made such a fuss at the hearing, the state put the matter off for study. In the meantime we collected money and began writing letters to alert people to what was going on [said Mrs. Edmiston]. Finally the state agreed to limit the herd to 250 head, authorizing the killing of any in excess of that number from 1961 to 1969. In 1969 we got the media to cover the "hunt," as it was called, and a lot of people got a look at what was going on. It was a real slaughter. They even used helicopters to herd the elk before the guns.

Mrs. Edmiston was on hand, helping reporters raise questions calculated to put state biologists on the spot. People began to take a second look at the situation, and then last October [1971] the state legislature, long prodded for action by Mrs. Edmiston and her group, passed a law to stop the slaughter of the Tule elk and restore the herd to two thousand in California. Legislation is now pending in Congress to make the elk habitat a national wildlife refuge.

"My personal philosophy," says Mrs. Edmiston," involves the belief that all life is sacred, and the survival of a species is an especially important thing. We wanted to save the Tule elk and other species on the land, to save their habitat, and to save open space wilderness and wildlife for the people."

"Enough Is Enough"

When a young lawyer, Wellborn Jack, Jr., of Shreveport, Louisiana, realized that the Gillham Dam project on the Arkansas Cossatot River would destroy the last free-flowing wild river in the Ouachita Mountain range of his region, he decided, "Enough is enough."

I was motivated to act primarily from a philosophical point of view. It was the endangered species approach. Our natural streams were endangered species in this region. Also, I felt the scenic value of the Cossatot River far outweighed the value of building another dam. This was the classic example of a bad dam.

The Army Corps of Engineers' Gillham Dam had been authorized by Congress in 1958 as part of a massive project involving the damming of the last six undammed rivers in the Ouachita range. There was little public opposition in the 1950s and construction moved ahead. But with growing public concern about the environment, response was strong when Wellborn Jack called for a stop to the construction of the last dam and reservoir on the Cossatot in late 1969.

A lawsuit was the farthest thing from our minds when we started [he said]. For a year we cajoled, badgered and requested the Engineers to suspend construction for an impartial environmental impact restudy and public hearings. We took the position that Congress had made a mistake in terms of today's standards.

Jack began his campaign to save the Cossatot by getting the Ozark Society, a regional conservation group, to take up the issue. He wrote an article about the Cossatot for the society newsletter. Then other organizations got involved, and soon the press was covering the controversy.

"We held a float-in to publicize our cause—with 102 canoes. We spoke and showed a film we had prepared to garden clubs and people in state and local government. The next thing you know we had a coalition of groups fighting the dam. But the Corps of Engineers ignored us."

Finally, in October 1970 the Environmental Defense Fund became involved and retained an Arkansas lawyer who filed for the coalition a suit against the project. Five months later the court ordered the project stopped. There have been recent indications that the Corps will attempt to revive the project, but the environmentalists are determined to preserve the river.

"Our strength lies in the fact that we are right and that we attract competent people to our cause," said Jack. "We are careful to be painstakingly accurate. There is a great deal of information around in the public domain, but you have to find it, dig it out."

The Man Who Never Gives Up

When he graduated from law school more than twenty years ago, hiking and outdoors enthusiast Wayne M. Harris of Rochester, New York, made a decision. "I felt that a person should make a contribution to society that was not done for monetary gain. And I found that the conservation field was one where I could do this important kind of service."

So lawyer Wayne Harris became a citizen pollution fighter. He continues to spend about twenty hours a week on his volunteer antipollution efforts. He has worked mainly through the Monroe County Conservation Council, of which he is a past president and now the chairman of its air and water pollution committee. Harris has successfully pushed for new laws and standards to control air, land and water pollution. He has harassed and cajoled public officials who don't do enough to abate pollution. He has instituted lawsuits against polluters. He and his family have collected and tested water samples and mapped outfall pipes that spew sewage into streams. And he has designed and directed a state-wide testing project to dramatize the water-pollution crisis.

Harris never gives up. A few years ago when his committee received complaints about an atomic reprocessing plant near Springville, New York, Harris got a geiger counter, went to the area, hiked through the woods, climbed fences, found the plant's outfall pipe, took readings, had tests made and was able to report to the proper authorities that the discharge was six thousand times over the limit prescribed by the Atomic Energy Commission.

Corrective action was not taken. So Harris began working through Senators Javits, Muskie and the late Robert F. Kennedy, and eventually got the AEC to direct the plant to reduce the amount of radioactive material in its discharges

In a more recent battle for tighter air-pollution laws Harris and other volunteers gave their own blood in tests they conducted in an auto-exhaust-filled garage.

In 1970 Harris realized a long-time dream with the establishment of Delta Laboratories, Inc., an independent environmental testing lab. Beholden to no industry or government agency, the lab is a place where environmentalists can obtain solid scientific evidence to support lawsuits and campaigns against polluters. Funds for the enterprise are raised largely through annual Walk for Water campaigns that Harris helps organize. Last year's walk [1971] drew five thousand participants, despite a snowstorm, and raised $72,000. Delta Labs now has three permanent employees and $150,000 worth of pollution-testing equipment.

Currently, Harris and his committee are also working to make politicians more concerned about environmental issues. Harris feels that many antipollution laws are too weak and that even when they have teeth, lawsuits can drag on interminably while pollution continues unabated. So his aim is to stir public ire against pollution and polluters by getting together all the facts in a case—with the aid of top-flight scientists who contribute their work and scores of other volunteers, especially young people.

"If you talk in general terms about lost beauty and how the rivers are full of junk, you'll get nowhere," said Harris. "To impress the politicians and bureaucrats, you need test results, expert witnesses, samples, photos, statistics."

"You Get Sick of Just Talking About It."

Two years ago, at a meeting of her Palo Alto, California, branch of the American Association of University Women, Mrs. Howard W. Harrington suggested a project for the year: Create an environmental handbook for housewives.

One year—and thousands of woman-hours—later, a paperback book with a foreword by Dr. Paul B. Sears, professor emeritus of conservation at Yale University, went to the printer (*If You Want To Save Your Environment . . . Start at Home! . . .*) Now, four printings later, Mrs. Harrington and her environmental handbook committee, still working out of their kitchens and some borrowed office space, have sold more than 75,000 copies of the little book (proceeds go to AAUW Fellowships Fund) in every state and over thirty foreign countries. Hawthorn Books, Inc., has a hard-cover edition.

Thirty-five women remain involved in the project. They spend a total of 150 hours a week answering mail, giving talks to area groups, keeping their accounts and mailing copies of their book in grocery bag wrapping paper and "recycled" cardboard boxes.

"Because we're involved at home, housewives get frustrated about working for the environment," says Carroll Harrington, "but we *can* do something about our environment. And our book shows how."

Similar thoughts occurred to a group of women in Washington, D.C. "There comes a point," said Mrs. Nancy Ignatius, "when you get sick of just talking about it and you do something."

It was after another of those dinner party conversations about cleaning up the environment that Mrs. Ignatius, whose husband is a former secretary of the Navy, and Mrs. Richard Helms, whose husband heads the nation's intelligence services, determined they would find a practical way to "utilize the vast woman-power of this country to help solve environmental problems."

They created an organization called Concern, Inc., and set about researching and preparing ecological shopping lists. Mrs. Ignatius expresses their reasoning this way: "Every time we go to the store, we have a choice, and that's a power that women can use for the good of the environment."

Their first shopping list, called *Eco-Tips,* was distributed to over fifty thousand people in the spring of 1970. Since then the growing number of volunteer workers at Concern, Inc., have produced two additional *Eco-Tips* guides . . . and an organic gardening calendar. . . .

NEW JOURNEY OF HOPE [6]

When this conference convened two weeks ago, the tasks before it seemed almost impossible of achievement. But it has faced up to the challenge—much of it controversial, all of it difficult, none of it with precedent for guidance—with a determination to find solutions.

The result is that it has dealt with all issues on its agenda —and it has dealt with them urgently, imaginatively and— above all—constructively.

Even in areas where agreements are lacking—and I must emphasize that these are few indeed—a major contribution has been made. For questions have been clarified, and a procedure has been started that, I am convinced, will ultimately lead to the agreement we seek.

But if we have reason for satisfaction—we have none for overconfidence.

We have taken the first steps on a new journey of hope for the future of mankind. But the journey before us is long and difficult, and we have barely begun it.

What is most important of all, however, is that we leave Stockholm with a program of action to cope with the critical relationships between the natural and the man-made systems of Planet Earth.

Mr. President, this conference was never conceived to be a once-and-for-all definitive approach to the problems of our global environment. For an inherent characteristic of the environmental issue is precisely that it will remain with us for an indefinite period.

And because it will, the fundamental task of the Stockholm conference has been to take the political decisions that will enable the community of nations to act together in a manner consistent with the Earth's physical interdependence.

This was our mandate. This is what we did.

[6] From address by Maurice F. Strong, Secretary General of the United Nations Conference on the Human Environment, June 16, 1972. *Only One Earth: Summary of the United Nations Conference on the Human Environment, Stockholm, 5-16 June, 1972.* United Nations Center for Economic and Social Information, Geneva. '72. p 21.

Declaration

We have approved a Declaration on the Human Environment. What many skeptics thought would only be a rhetorical statement has become a highly significant document reflecting a community of interest among nations regardless of politics, ideologies or economic status. Despite the difficulties and the differences that emerged—the very fact that delegates labored as they have testifies to the importance their governments attach to the Declaration and—to the very basic principle of our age of environment—that of every nation's responsibility to ensure that activities within their jurisdiction or control do not cause damage to the environment of other states or of areas beyond the limits of national jurisdiction.

We have approved a wide-ranging Action Plan which, with its Earthwatch Program of global assessment and monitoring, its Environmental Management Activities, and its Supporting Measures, constitutes a turning point in man's endeavors to preserve and protect his planetary heritage.

We have approved both the establishment of continuing environmental machinery within the United Nations and the provision of necessary financing—including a $100 million Environment Fund to give it the life it must have if our actions here are to have any lasting meaning.

We have approved the substance of an Ocean Dumping Convention that will be finalized before November [1972] and opened for signature this year.

Action Plan

Mr. President, we have done all this—and more. As part of the Action Plan, we have set into motion machinery that will:

—drastically curtail emission into the atmosphere of chlorinated hydrocarbons and heavy metals
—provide information about possible harmful effects of various activities before these activities are initiated

—accelerate research to better assess the risk of climatic modification and open up consultations among those concerned
—assist developing countries to cope with the urban crisis
   and its related priority needs such as housing and water
   supply and waste disposal
—intensify the preparation of conventions on conservation
   for the protection of the world's natural and cultural
   heritage
—stress the priority of education and information to enable
   people to weigh the decisions which shape their future
   and to create a wider sense of responsibility
—initiate steps to protect and manage common resources
   considered of unique value to the world community
—initiate a global program to ensure genetic resources for
   future generations
—create an International Referral Service that will enable
   nations to exchange environmental information and
   knowledge
—incorporate environmental considerations into the review
   of the development strategies embodied in the Second
   Development Decade [the seventies]
—pursue regional cooperation for purposes of financial and
   technical assistance
—prevent environmental considerations from becoming pre-
   texts to limit trade or impose barriers against developing-
   country exports
—emphasize opportunities that environmental concerns open
   up for developing countries, including the possible re-
   location of industries to countries whose natural systems
   have been less burdened
—study the financing of additional costs to developing countries arising from environmental considerations

These few examples are not all-inclusive. They merely
illustrate the rich variety and scope of the actions that were
taken here. And, of course, they do not include the many

vital proposals that were referred to governments for their consideration and attention as appropriate.

Unanimity

This conference has pronounced itself—and when the General Assembly meets again it will have before it concrete evidence that the governments represented here fully mean what they have said: Their unanimous recommendation for the establishment of the ongoing United Nations environmental machinery and the necessary initial funding.

And it is my hope that, when the General Assembly takes action on this vital recommendation, all countries will play their full role, whether or not they have been here in Stockholm with us.

Mr. President, we have earned the right to a moment of self-congratulation, at the close of this historic conference. But we must not allow this mood to delude us about the ability of established governments and international agencies to bring about the changes that must take place or to carry through on our decisions without the active participation of many groups outside the official structures of governance.

An unprecedented degree of public interest in our preparations and now in our present deliberation has been demonstrated by the presence here of nearly 1,500 representatives of the mass media and more than 700 accredited observers from nongovernmental organizations. These voluntary, professional and scientific organizations along with press, radio and television have all served to alert governments and inform the public about present and future environmental perils and in so doing they have focused the world spotlight on our work.

Nongovernmental organizations in particular have stimulated a two-way exchange of ideas and information that have made major contributions to the success of our deliberations. I now look forward to their initiatives and cooperation in the future environmental work of the UN.

Mr. President, I believe we must now actively seek to broaden the base of decision making in environmental affairs. We must add a new dimension to the discourse between governments and peoples, engaging the best technological and managerial abilities of the entire world. The global environment has a global constituency. The community of the concerned is now no less than the world community.

I believe we must leave here with an awakened sense of this new dynamic breaching the barriers between those who make the official decisions and those who are affected by such decisions. If we do that, it may well have a more far-reaching impact on the affairs of Planet Earth than any of the more technical decisions we have reached in the course of the conference.

But the need for technical solutions has not circumscribed our view. This conference has emphasized both in word and in deed that deep and pervasive changes are needed in the way man looks at his world, at the role of man within nature, and at his relations with other men.

It has asserted its conviction that man cannot manage his relations with nature unless he learns to manage better the relations between man and man—that if he is to preserve Planet Earth for future generations, he must also make it a better home for present generations.

The force of this conviction was an imperative in our deliberations, and we can but hope now that out of it will come a new burst of political will to end, finally, the massive poverty which still exists in a world of unprecedented plenty, and which still comprises the greatest barrier dividing the tribes of man—a barrier which must be bridged if we are to achieve the degree of cooperation needed to secure the future for mankind.

Mr. President, this Stockholm conference has done more than recognize the urgent need for a change in man's priorities. It has achieved a heartening consensus to the effect that no fundamental conflict exists between the goal of environmental quality on the one hand and economic and social progress on the other.

Global Unity

So there *is* reason for hope in the work it has done—in the programs it has adopted—in the awareness it has expressed of our global unity—in the affirmation that the problems of the human environment can only be resolved if we place man at the center of our concerns—and in the conviction that we must liberate ourselves from the outdated and outworn habits of the past.

Mr. President, I believe that, as we leave now, we must do so with determination to build on the foundations we have laid here in Stockholm. If we do not, then this conference will have been a brief flash, a meteor burning its way through the blackness of space.

And I believe that we *will* build together—that we *will* continue together to work for the achievement of the larger, richer future which the collective will and energies of mankind can shape—that we *will* together continue our long journey towards a creative and dynamic harmony for all life on Planet Earth.

I believe we will because this conference has demonstrated that the United Nations *is* at the heart of our troubled turbulent world. It has demonstrated that, if governments give it their support and cooperation, it *can* and *will* play a vital role in bringing harmony into the relationship between man and the natural systems which support his life.

And if it does, perhaps then it is not too much to hope that it *can* and *will* fulfill the hopes of the Charter and inspire a peaceful and just world community in which diverse states and people cooperate for the common good of all mankind.

BIBLIOGRAPHY

An asterisk (*) preceding a reference indicates that the article or a part of it has been reprinted in this book.

BOOKS, PAMPHLETS, AND DOCUMENTS

Adams, Ruth. Say no! Rodale Press. '71.

Albertson, Peter and Barnett, Margery, eds. Managing the planet. Prentice-Hall. '72.

An abridgment of *Environment and society in transition*; a symposium. New York Academy of Science. '71.

Atkinson, Brooks. This bright land: a personal view. Natural History Press. '72.

Published for the American Museum of Natural History.

Barnet, H. J. and Morse, Chandler. Scarcity and growth; the economics of natural resource availability. Resources for the Future; Oxford University Press. '63.

Behan, R. W. and Weddle, R. M. eds. Ecology, economics, environment. School of forestry, University of Montana. '71.

Cailliet, G. M. and others. Everyman's guide to ecological living. Macmillan. '71.

Caldwell, L. K. Environment: a challenge for modern society. Natural History Press. '70.

Published for the American Museum of Natural History.

Caldwell, L. K. In defense of earth; international protection of the biosphere Indiana University Press. '72.

Caras, R. A. Last chance on earth; a requiem for wildlife. Schocken. '72.

Carson, R. L. Silent spring. Houghton. '62.

Caudill, H. M. My land is dying. Dutton. '71.

Commoner, Barry. Closing circle. Knopf. '71.

Excerpt. Today's Education. 61:42-5. Mr. '72. Breaking the law of ecology.

Concern, Inc. Eco-Tips [ecological shopping guide]. Concern, Inc. 2233 Wisconsin Av. N.W. Washington, D.C. 20007.

Cooley, R. A. and Wandesforde-Smith, Geoffrey, eds. Congress and the environment. University of Washington Press. '70.

Crenson, M. A. The un-politics of air pollution: a study of non-decision-making in the cities. Johns Hopkins Press. '71.

Dasmann, R. F. Environmental conservation. 2d ed. Wiley. '68.

Davies, J. C. 3d. The politics of pollution. Pegasus. '70.

Day, J. A. and others. Dimensions of the environmental crisis. Wiley. '71.

Dubos, R. J. A god within. Scribner. '72.
   Excerpt. Audubon. 74:106-7. Mr. '72. Pursuit of absurdity.

Dubos, R. J. Man, medicine, and environment. Praeger. '68.

Dworsky, L. B. Pollution; with an introduction by Stewart L. Udall. (Conservation in the United States; a documentary history) Chelsea House Publishers; Van Nostrand-Reinhold. '71.

*Ecologist, Editors of. Blueprint for survival. Houghton. '72.
   Reprinted in this volume: Excerpts from "Introduction: The Need for Change," as it appeared in *Ecologist.* 2:2-6. Ja. '72.

Ewald, W. R. Jr. ed. Environment and change: the next fifty years. Indiana University Press. '68.
   Based on papers commissioned for the American Institute of Planners' 2-year consultation, pt. 1: Optimum environment with man as the measure; Portland, Oregon, August 14-18, 1966.
   Title of 1967 edition: Environment for man.

Ewald, W. R. Jr. ed. Environment and policy; the next fifty years. Indiana University Press. '68.
   Based on papers commissioned for the American Institute of Planners' 2-year consultation, pt. 2: The Washington conference, October 1-6, 1967.

Falk, R. A. This endangered planet; prospects and proposals for human survival. Random House. '71.

Fallows, J. M. The water lords; Ralph Nader's study group report on industry and environmental crisis in Savannah, Georgia. Grossman Publishers. '71.

Fanning, Odom. Opportunities in environmental careers. Vocational Guidance. '71.
   Excerpts. Saturday Review. 54:60. My. 1, '71. Environment boom.

*Foreign Policy Association. Great decisions 1973. The Association. 345 E. 46th St. New York 10017. '73.
   Reprinted in this volume: Fact Sheet No. 6. Man on earth: can he control his environment. p 65-6.

Frakes, G. E. and Solberg, C. B. eds. Pollution papers. Appleton. '71.

Goldman, M. I. Controlling pollution; the economics of a cleaner America. Prentice-Hall. '67.

Grad, F. P. and others. Environmental control: priorities, policies, and the law. Columbia University Press. '71.

Graham, Frank. Since Silent spring. Houghton. '70.

Great Britain. Royal Commission on Environmental Pollution. First report; Sir Eric Ashby, chairman. H.M.S.O. Box 569. London, S.E. 1. '71.

Harrington, Carroll and others. If you want to save your environment . . . start at home. Hawthorn. '71; paper ed. '70. The author. Am. Assn. of Univ. Women. 774 Gailen Court. Palo Alto, Calif. 94303.

Harrison, G. A. Earthkeeping: the war with nature and a proposal for peace. Houghton. '71.

Helfrich, H. W. Jr. ed. The environmental crisis. Yale University Press. '70. 2v.
> V 1: Man's struggle to live with himself; V 2: Agenda for survival.

Hill, Gladwin. Our troubled waters: the fight against water pollution. (Public Affairs Pamphlet No 462) Public Affairs Committee. 381 Park Av. S. New York 10016. '71.

Johnson, C. E. ed. Eco-crisis. Wiley. '70.

Kormondy, E. J. Concepts of ecology. Prentice-Hall. '69.

Laycock, George. The diligent destroyers. Doubleday. '70.

Linton, R. M. Terracide: America's destruction of her living environment. Little. '70.

Love, G. A. and Love, R. M. eds. Ecological crisis; readings for survival. Harcourt. '70.

McHarg, I. L. Design with nature. Natural History Press. '69.
> Published for the American Museum of Natural History.

Meadows, D. H. and others. The limits to growth; a report from the Club of Rome's Project on the Predicament of Mankind. Universe Books. '72.
> *Excerpts*: On reaching a state of global equilibrium. New York *Times*. p 35. Mr. 13, '72.
> *Comment*. Time. 99:32+. Ja. 24, '72. Worst is yet to be?
> *Editorial comment*: Questions must be raised about the imminence of the disaster. Leonard Silk. New York *Times*. p 35. Mr. 13; p 43. Mr. 14, '72.

Mignon, M. R. comp. Our polluted planet; a bibliography of government publications on pollution and the environment. Western Washington State College. '71.

Mines, Samuel. The last days of mankind: ecological survival or extinction. Simon & Schuster. '71.

Mitchell, J. G. and Stallings, C. L. eds. Ecotactics; the Sierra Club handbook for environment activists. Pocket Books. '70.

Neuhaus, R. J. In defense of people; ecology and the seduction of radicalism. Macmillan. '71.

Nicholson, Max. The environmental revolution; a guide for the new masters of the world. McGraw. '70.

Princeton University. Woodrow Wilson School of Public and International Affairs. Center of International Studies. Ecology and politics in America's environmental crisis; proceedings of conference held at Princeton, March 1970. (Policy memorandum no 37) The Center. Princeton, N.J. 08540. '70.

Ramparts, Editors of. Eco-catastrophe. Harper. '70.

Perin, Constance. With man in mind: an interdisciplinary prospectus for environmental design. MIT Press. '70.
> *Review*: Architectural Forum. 135:16. D. '71. Samuel Kaplan.

Ridgeway, James. The politics of ecology. Dutton. '70.
    Review. Natural History. 80:102+. F. '71. E. F. Roberts.
Rockefeller, N. A. Our environment can be saved. Doubleday. '70.
Saltonstall, Richard. Your environment and what you can do about
    it. Walker. '70.
Sangster, R. P. Ecology: a selected bibliography. Council of Plan-
    ning Librarians. P.O. Box 229. Monticello, Ill. 61856. '71.
Sax, J. L. Defending the environment; a strategy for citizen action.
    Knopf. c'71.
    Reviews. Natural History. 80:103-5. F. '71. G. M. Woodwell; Science.
    172:47-8. Ap. 2, '71. H. P. Green.
Terry, Mark. Teaching for survival. Ballantine Books. '71.
    Excerpts. Natural History. 80:6-8+. Ja. '71. Hello Ents, good-bye
    Aristotle.
Theobald, Robert. Habit and habitat. Prentice-Hall. '72.
United Nations. Office of Public Information. The human environ-
    ment: new challenge for the United Nations. The Office. New
    York 10017. '71.
*United Nations Conference on the Human Environment, 1972.
    Only one earth; summary of the conference, Stockholm, 5-16
    June, 1972. United Nations Center for Economic and Social
    Information, Geneva. '72.
    Reprinted in this volume: New journey of hope; address by Maurice
    F. Strong. p 21.
United States. Council on Environmental Quality. Ocean dumping:
    a national policy. Supt. of Docs. Washington, D.C. 20402. '70.
United States. Council on Environmental Quality. The President's
    1971 environmental program. Supt. of Docs. Washington, D.C.
    20402. '71.
United States. Department of Agriculture. Managing our environ-
    ment: a report on ways agricultural research fights pollution.
    Supt. of Docs. Washington, D.C. 20402. '71.
United States. Department of Housing and Urban Development.
    Environment and the community: an annotated bibliography.
    Supt. of Docs. Washington, D.C. 20402. '71.
United States. Department of State. Secretary of State's Advisory
    Committee on 1972 United Nation's Conference on Human
    Environment. Stockholm and beyond; report. (Publication
    8657) Supt. of Docs. Washington, D.C. 20402. '72.
United States. Environmental Health Service. Proceedings of the
    first invitational conference on health research in housing and
    its environment, Airlie House, Warrenton, Virginia, March
    17-19, 1970. The Service. Rockville, Md. 20852. '71.
United States. Executive Office of the President. Office of Science
    and Technology. Protecting the world environment in the
    light of population increase: a report to the President. Supt.
    of Docs. Washington, D.C. 20402. '70.

United States. House of Representatives. Committee on Education and Labor. Select Subcommittee on Education. Environmental quality education act of 1970: hearings, March 24-May 2, 1970, on H.R. 14753, a bill to authorize the United States Commissioner of Education to establish educational programs to encourage understanding of policies and support of activities designed to enhance environmental quality and maintain biological balance. 91st Congress, 2d session. Supt. of Docs. Washington, D.C. 20402. '70.

United States. House of Representatives. Committee on Merchant Marine and Fisheries. Subcommittee on Fisheries and Wildlife Conservation. Administration of the National environmental policy act: hearings, December 7-22, 1970, on Federal agency compliances with Section 102(2) (C) and Section 103 of the National environmental policy act of 1969. 91st Congress, 2d session. Supt. of Docs. Washington, D.C. 20402. '71.

United States. House of Representatives. Committee on Merchant Marine and Fisheries. Subcommittee on Fisheries and Wildlife Conservation. Council on environmental quality: hearings, March 5 and August 12, 1970. 91st Congress, 2d session. Supt. of Docs. Washington, D.C. 20402. '70.

United States. House of Representatives. Committee on Merchant Marine and Fisheries. Subcommittee on Fisheries and Wildlife Conservation. Environmental data bank: hearings, June 2-26, 1970, on H.R. 17436, H.R. 17779, H.R. 18141, bills to amend the National environmental policy act of 1969, to provide for a national environmental data bank. 91st Congress, 2d session. Supt. of Docs. Washington, D.C. 20402. '70.

United States. House of Representatives. Committee on Public Works. Laws of the United States relating to water pollution control and environmental quality. 91st Congress, 2d session. The Committee. Washington, D.C. 20515. '70.

United States. National Industrial Pollution Control Council. Electric and Nuclear Sub-Council. Self-analysis of pollution problems; report. Supt. of Docs. Washington, D.C. 20402. '71.

United States. Office of Science and Technology. Energy Policy Staff. Electric power and the environment; a report. Supt. of Docs. Washington, D.C. 20402. '70.

United States. Senate. Committee on Commerce. Subcommittee on Energy, Natural Resources, and the Environment. Environmental protection act of 1970: hearings on S. 3575, May 12-July 10, 1970. 91st Congress, 2d session. Supt. of Docs. Washington, D.C. 20402. '70.

United States. Senate. Committee on Government Operations. Subcommittee on Intergovernmental Relations. Intergovernmental coordination of power development and Environmental protection act: hearings, pts. 1-2, February 3-June 15, 1970, on S. 2752, to promote intergovernmental cooperation in the control of site selection and construction of bulk power facilities for environmental and coordination purposes. 91st Congress, 2d session. Supt. of Docs. Washington, D.C. 20402. '70-'71.

United States. Senate. Committee on Interior and Insular Affairs. Congress and the nation's environment: environmental affairs of the 91st Congress; prepared by the Environmental policy division, Congressional research service, Library of Congress. Supt. of Docs. Washington, D.C. 20402. '71.

United States. Senate. Committee on Interior and Insular Affairs. First annual environmental quality report: hearing, August 13, 1970. 91st Congress, 2d session. Supt. of Docs. Washington, D.C. 20402. '70.

United States. Senate. Committee on Interior and Insular Affairs. Law and the environment: selected materials on tax exempt status and public interest litigation. 91st Congress, 2d session. The Committee. Washington, D.C. 20515. '70.

United States. Senate. Committee on Labor and Public Welfare. Subcommittee on Education. Environmental quality education act: hearings, May 19 and 20, 1970, on S. 3151 [and other bills]. 91st Congress, 2d session. Supt. of Docs. Washington, D.C. 20402. '70.

United States. Senate. Committee on Public Works. National environmental laboratories: a compilation of comments and materials related to a proposed environmental laboratory. 92d Congress, 1st session. The Committee. Washington, D.C. 20515. '71.

United States. Senate. Committee on Public Works. Some environmental implications of national fuels policies; report, by Walter G. Planet. The Committee. Washington, D.C. 20515. '70.

United States. Senate. Committee on Public Works. Subcommittee on Air and Water Pollution. Report of the Council on Environmental Quality: hearing, August 11, 1970, for the purpose of providing open discussion of the findings and recommendations of the President's Council on Environmental Quality. 91st Congress, 2d session. Supt. of Docs. Washington, D.C. 20402. '70.

United States. Senate. Committee on Public Works. Subcommittee on Roads. National environmental policy act relative to highways: hearing, August 25, 1970, on implementation of the National environmental policy act as it relates to the planning and construction of highways. 91st Congress, 2d session. Supt. of Docs. Washington, D.C. 20402. '70.

Wagner, R. H. Environment and man. Norton. '71.

Ward, Barbara (Lady Jackson), and Dubos, René. Only one earth: the care and maintenance of a small planet. Norton. '72.

Warner, A. W. and others, eds. The environment of change. Columbia University Press. '69.

PERIODICALS

American Bar Association Journal. 57:127-31. F. '71. Tax incentives don't stop pollution. A. W. Reitze and Glenn Reitze.

American City. 86:74+. Mr. '71. Needed, world-wide environment solutions; United auto workers and the United Nations explore pollution problems. Stella Margold.

American City. 86:62. Ap. '71. Nature worst water polluter.

American Economic Review. 61:153-77. My. '71. Environmental pollution: economics and policy. A. V. Kneese.

American Economic Review. 61:392-421. My. '71. Population and environment in the United States [three conference papers, with discussion].

American Education. 7:inside cover, 6-10. My. '71. Environmental education cannot wait [with editorial comment]. S. P. Marland, Jr.

American Education. 8:26-30. Ja. '72. Earth day year around; Ecology center, inc. of Ann Arbor. Judith Serrin.

American Education. 8:31. Ja. '72. Support for environmental education.

American Forests. 77:24-7+. Mr. '71. Even in Siberia it's the age of ecology. Ron Richardson.

American Forests. 77:16-19+. My. '71. New assertion of rights. Richard Pardo.

American Forests. 77:32-5+. Je. '71. Conservationists go to court. R. D. Butcher.

American Forests. 78:16-19. Mr. '72. Environmentalism: fad or fixture. Clay Schoenfeld.

American Heritage. 22:65-9+. O. '71. Urban pollution: many long years ago. J. A. Tarr.

American Industrial Development Journal. 6:1-11. Ap. '71. Is a no-growth economy the answer to environmental pollution? L. F. Smith.

American West. 9:44-7+. Ja. '72. Our frontier heritage and the environment. L. E. Oliva.

American West. 9:36-41. Mr. '72. Can we save our wild places from our civilized public? national parks in jeopardy. R. M. Pyle.

Annals of the American Academy of Political and Social Science. 400:103-15. Mr. '72. Environmental quality as an administrative problem. L. K. Caldwell.

Architectural Record. 151:111-12. F. '72. Environmental responsibility of the architect. M. O. Urbahn.

Audubon. 74:104. Mr. '72. Which way to water quality? R. K. Davis.

Aviation Week & Space Technology. 94:11. Ap. 12, '71. Ecological problem. Robert Hotz.

Better Homes & Gardens. 49:30. Ap, 20+. My, 28+. Je, 4+. Jl, 12+. Ag, 34+. S. '71. Environment yes, hysteria no.

Better Homes & Gardens. 49:20+. My. '71. Sewage pollution: what can be done and when?

Bulletin of the Atomic Scientists. 26:17-20. Ja. '70. To trouble a star; the cost of intervention in nature. Garrett Hardin.

> *Reply with rejoinder.* Bulletin of the Atomic Scientists. 27:2-4. Ap. '71. R. B. Coffman.

Bulletin of the Atomic Scientists. 27:36-40. My. '71. Destruction of Indochina; report of Stanford biology study group.

Bulletin of the Atomic Scientists. 28:5-8. Ja. '72. Living dangerously in the age of science. Eugene Rabinowitch.

Bulletin of the Atomic Scientists. 28:5-10. F. '72. Interaction of man and the environment [adaptation of address, July 1971]. E. K. Fedorov.

Bulletin of the Atomic Scientists. 28:5-8+. Mr. '72. Global effects of increased use of energy. A. M. Weinberg and R. P. Hammond.

Business Week. p 104-5+. Ja. 16, '71. New target in the antipollution drive [sewage treatment].

> *Editorial comment:* Business Week. p 112. Ja. 16, '71. Cities as polluters.

*Business Week. p 72-3+. Ja. 23, '71. Trade collides with ecology.

Business Week. p 18-19. My. 8, '71. Clean air act cuts more teeth.

Business Week. p 46. My. 15, '71. Polluters raise the cleanup ante.

Business Week. p 20-1. Jl. 3, '71. Delaware's new Keep Out sign; law banning heavy industrial facilities from the Delaware coast.

Business Week. p 35. Jl. 10, '71. Cleanup collides with the GNP [Netherlands].

Business Week. p 70-1. F. 5, '72. Stormy debate over zero discharge.

Camping Magazine. 43:5. Je. '71. Ecology: is it a fad? J. J. Kirk.

Ceres. 4:27-30. Mr./Ap. '71. Africa is still in time: a sick environment is not only the privilege of the rich. G. E. A. Lardner.

*Changing Times. 26:6-11. Mr. '72. What can you do to clean up the environment? Plenty!

Chemistry. 44:6-15. O. '71. Haste makes waste; pollution and entropy. H. A. Bent.
  Discussion with rejoinder. Chemistry. 45:30-1. F. '72.

Christian Century. 88:195-7. F. 10, '71. Herbicides in Vietnam: violating the laws, starving our allies. C.-G. McDaniel.

Christian Century. 88:613. My. 19, '71. Air power and the environmentalists.

*Christian Science Monitor. p 1-2. My. 26, '72. Ecology treaty: full of potential. P. C. Stuart.

*Christian Science Monitor. p 7. My. 31, '72. What is man doing to East Africa? R. C. Cowen.

Christianity Today. 16:22-3. Mr. 31, '72. Ecology: dying to live again.

*Commentary. 52:4+. O. '71. Doomsday fears & modern life. Norman Podhoretz.

Commonweal. 94:27-8. Mr. 19, '71. Having it both ways [business as usual and environment restored].

Commonweal. 94:226. My. 14, '71. Proliferating at home; thermal pollution. John Deedy.

Commonweal. 94:324-5. Je. 25, '71. Hardhats, hyacinths and returnable bottles. R. W. Gibbons.

Commonweal. 95:195. N. 26, '71. Politics and pollution.

Congressional Digest. 49:193-224. Ag./S. '70. The question of the Federal role in pollution control: pros & cons.

Congressional Quarterly Weekly Report. 29:367. F. 12, '71. The environment: proposed taxes, laws and research.

Conservationist. 25:4-5. F. '71. Getting started: environmental action in the community. C. C. Morrison, Jr.

Conservationist. 26:3. F. '72. Reveille for bold spirits.

Current. 128:34-9. Ap. '71. Is man over adapting to his environment? R. J. Dubos.
  Original article in February 1971 issue of Psychology Today.

Current. 129:39-46. My. '71. Are we about to plunder Alaska. Richard Pollak.
  Original article entitled "Plunder of Alaska" in March 1971 issue of Progressive.

Current History. 59:73-81+. Ag. '70. The costs of fighting pollution. M. I. Goldman.

*Current History. 59:82-3+. Ag. '70. The Federal Government and the environment. G. S. McGovern.

Department of State Bulletin. 64:67-70. Ja. 11, '71. United Nations adopts resolution on human environment conference; statement, December 7, 1970; with text of resolution. Claiborne Pell.

Department of State Bulletin. 64:77. Ja. 18, '71. Use of herbicides in Viet-Nam to be phased out; White House announcement, December 26, 1970.

Department of State Bulletin. 64:334-9. Mr. 15, '71. U.S. initiatives for the 1972 U.N. conference on the human environment; statement, February 9, 1971. C. A. Herter, Jr.

Department of State Bulletin. 64:831-2. Je. '28, '71. Second United States-Japan meeting on pollution held at Washington; joint communiqué, June 2, 1971.

Department of State Bulletin. 65:21-2. Jl. 5, '71. Environment and development; the interlocking problems; remarks, May 24, 1971. G. H. W. Bush.

Department of State Bulletin. 66:544. Ap. 10, '72. Department sponsors conference on effects of population growth.

*Department of State Bulletin. 67:106-12. Jl. 24, '72. Statement by Mr. [Russell E.] Train [before the UN Conference on the Human Environment, Stockholm, June 6, 1972].

Economic Quarterly Review. p 5-12. Mr. '71. Seven methods of anti-pollution policy: an essay in taxonomy. J. Pen.

*Economist. 236:40+, 43-4. S. 5, '70. Pollution: the Swedes come clean; Italy: sewage in your eye; Japan: where it comes down in chunks; Russia: it's no better over there.

Economist. 239:47-8. Ap. 24, '71. Washing dirty water.

Editorial Research Reports. v 1 no 1:3-24. Ja. 6, '71. Pollution technology. H. B. Shaffer.

Education Digest. 36:9-12. F. '71. Challenge of environmental education. J. A. Wagar.

Environment. 13:34-43. Mr. '71. Tour of Vietnam. Terri Aaronson.

Environment. 13:2-19. Ap. '71. Causes of pollution. Barry Commoner and others.

Environment. 13:20-4+. Jl. '71. Cloud on the desert. Roy Craig.

Environment. 13:10-17. O. '71. Pollution of Asia: report of the Conference on Asian environments. M. T. Farvar and others.

Farm Journal. 95:37. My. '71. Farm bureau steps up environmental crusade. Dick Seim.

Field & Stream. 75:24. Ja. '71. Environmental Action group.

Field & Stream. 75:12+. F. '71. Legal strategies for environmental control. Steve Lawrence.

Field & Stream. 76:46+. My. '71. House at the crossroads. Michael Frome.

Field & Stream. 76:34. Jl. '71. Environmental action line. Michael Frome.

*Forbes. 107:22-4+. Je. 15, '71. Fellow Americans, keep out! [regional isolationism]

Foreign Affairs. 50:325-38. Ja. '72. Pollution: precedent and prospect. C. C. Humpstone.

*Fortune. 82:112-15+. O. '70. The long, littered path to clean air and water. Gene Bylinsky.

Fortune. 83:110-13. Ja. '71. Metallic menaces in the environment. Gene Bylinsky.

Harper's Magazine. 242:20+. F. '71. Survival U is alive and burgeoning in Green Bay, Wisconsin. John Fischer.

Harper's Magazine. 243:100-5. O. '71. Not nature alone. Richard Neuhaus.

*Harper's Magazine. 244:66-71. Ja. '72. Saving the crusade. P. F. Drucker.

Harvard Business Review. 49:148-50+. Jl. '71. Case of the offending effluent. Ram Charan and Nicola Wormald.

Horticulture. 49:30-3+. My. '71. Environmental dilemma. P. E. Waggoner.

House & Garden. 139:49+. Je. '71. Here's how eight individuals are helping to improve our environment. Beverly Russell.

Human Ecology Forum. 1:3-7. Winter '71. Phosphates and the environment: two ecosystems. Simone Clemhout.

Industrial Development and Manufacturers Record. 139:1-9. N./D. '70. Fifty legislative climates turn stormy as states fire up pollution control programs.

International Social Science Journal. 22:563-725. N. 4, '70. Controlling the human environment.

Japan Quarterly. 18:162-7. Ap./Je. '71. Pollution and local government. Kunimoto Yoshiro.

Journal of Economic Issues. 5:26-46. Mr. '71. Environmental control at the crossroads. Harold Wolozin.

*Journal of Forestry. 69:12-16. Ja. '71. A critical appraisal of the environmental movement. R. S. Boster.

Life. 70:30-5. Mr. 5, '71. Clean-up mood sweeps the nations.

Life. 70:34. Ap. 9, '71. Erasing grown-up vandalism.

Life. 71:58-64. N. 26, '71. Goodbye to you, blue Hawaii.

Life. 72:28. Ja. 28, '72. Won't anybody hear the awful truth? Loudon Wainwright.

Living Wilderness. 35:25-30. Summer '71. Case against the disaster lobby; address, January 28, 1971. T. R. Shepard, Jr.
    Reply: Living Wilderness. 35:36-8. Autumn '71. The disaster lobby revisited. Casey Bukro.

Living Wilderness. 35:19-20. Autumn '71. Who ate tomorrow? address, November 10, 1971. N. P. Reed.

McCall's. 98:42. Mr. '71. If it stinks, stop it; Long Island environmental council. James Egan.

McCall's. 99:52. O. '71. To catch a polluter. Marjorie Palmer.

Missouri Law Review. 36:78-104. Winter '71. Environmental law: new legal concepts in the antipollution fight. P. E. Murphy.

Monthly Labor Review. 94:3-13. N. '71. Economic growth and ecology: a biologist's view. Barry Commoner.

Monthly Labor Review. 94:14-21. N. '71. Economic growth and ecology: an economist's view. W. W. Heller.

Nation. 213:358-61. O. 18, '71. Has the environment a future? M. I. Goldman.

Nation. 214:492-6. Ap. 17, '72. Not quite dead: the pathology of Lake Erie. Quincy Dadisman.

National Geographic. 141:1-27. Ja. '72. Imperiled Everglades. Fred Ward.

National Parks & Conservation Magazine. 45:2. Ja. '71. World heritage. A. W. Smith.

National Parks & Conservation Magazine. 45:6-9. Ap. '71. Youth, rebellion & the environment.

National Parks & Conservation Magazine. 45:15-19. S. '71. Planet earth under the occupation. D. L. Allen.

National Parks & Conservation Magazine. 45:9-13. O. '71. Hawaii; haven for endangered species? Warren King.

National Parks & Conservation Magazine. 46:I-IV. Ja. '72. Profit motive and the environment; address, October 12, 1971. A. W. Smith.

National Westminster Bank Quarterly Review. p 43-52. My. '71. Economics and the environment. H. W. Richardson.

National Wildlife. 9:5-9. Ap. '71. We tried to live the EQ way. Phyllis Feldkamp; Roslyn Rosen.

National Wildlife. 9:17-20. Je. '71. This country is on fire [interview with Ralph Nader; ed. by Lynn Langway].

National Wildlife. 10:42-3. F. '72. How nature keeps its balance. A. R. Chalfant.

National Wildlife. 10:18-19. Ap. '72. What America really thinks about pollution cleanup; report of special Gallup survey.

*Nation's Business. 59:30-3. Ap. '71. Exaggeration: the other pollution peril [interview]. Philip Handler.

Natural History. 80:56-61. Mr. '71. Ecocide in Indochina. A. H. Westing.

Natural History. 81:20+. Ja. '72. Letter from a farmer: respect for the land [with biographical sketch]. J. O. Harvey.

New Republic. 164:9-10. Je. 19, '71. Environment and the bureaucracy; Hart-McGovern bill. J. L. Sax.

New Republic. 165:9-10. D. 25, '71. Hold your nose; Administration fighting to defeat bills.
   Reply with rejoinder. New Republic. 166:34-5. Ja. 15, '72. R. E. Train. 166:5-7. Ja. 22, '72.

*New York Review of Books. 17:18-27. N. 18, '71. Man the pest: The dim chance of survival. S. R. Eyre.

*New York Times. p 24. Jl. 8, '71. Nation's energy crisis: is unbridled growth indispensable to the good life? J. N. Wilford.

New York Times. p 29. F. 12, '72. A world without growth? H. C. Wallich.
   Reply: Growth and survival. H. V. Hodson. New York *Times.* p 43. Mr. 8, '72.

New York Times. p 1+. Mr. 13, '72. Curbs on pollution costly but feasible industry is advised. E. W. Kenworthy.

New York Times. p 1+. Mr. 26, '72. Panel urges curb on cities' growth. Jack Rosenthal.

New York Times. p 5F. Je. 4, '72. Cost of cleanup; or, a myth of factory closings is exploded. Gladwin Hill.

New York Times. p 1+. S. 2, '72. U.S.-Soviet pact sets up projects on environment. Hedrick Smith.

New York Times Magazine. p 28-9+. My. 23, '71. Return of Charles Lindbergh. Alden Whitman.

*New York Times Magazine. p 40-2+. N. 21, '71. The Luddites were not all wrong. Wade Greene and Soma Golden.

New Yorker. 48:45-6+. Je. 3, '72. Environmentalist [profile of Maurice F. Strong]. E. J. Kahn, Jr.

Newsweek. 77:72+. Ap. 26, '71. Nader's waders.

Newsweek. 77:87. Je. 7, '71. Environment vs. poverty. H. C. Wallich.

Newsweek. 78:55. Jl. 5, '71. Delaware: nature over industry.

Newsweek. 79:102-3. Mr. 13, '72. To grow or not to grow.

Newsweek. 79:62+. Ap. 3, '72. Pipe dreams? Interior department report on trans-Alaskan pipeline.

Ohio State Law Journal. 32:16-42. Winter '71. Air pollution—expanding citizens remedies. J. W. Van Doren.

Orbis. 14:490-9. Summer '70. Challenges to the environment: some international implications. Livingston Hartley.

Organic Gardening and Farming. 18:114-18. Mr. '71. Putting PEP into fighting pollution: pollution and environmental problems. Armand Ferrara.

Organic Gardening and Farming. 18:77-80. Ap. '71. Adversary scientists & agricultural renegades. Jerome Goldstein.

Outdoor Life. 147:46-7+. Je. '71. What one man can do.

Parents Magazine & Better Family Living. 46:54-5+. Mr. '71. Our family fights pollution. J. R. Coggins and D.-E. Coggins.

Parks & Recreation. 6:22-4+. Mr. '71. Congressional flight on a
  fragile spacecraft. L. K. Lee.
Physics Today. 24:9. F. '71. Back-to-nature movement a threat?
  [letter]. John Boardman.
    Editorial comment. Physics Today. 24:80. F. '71. H. L. Davis.
Physics Today. 25:101-3. Mr. '72. Environmental program is under
  way at LBL [Lawrence Berkeley Laboratory of the University
  of California].
Popular Electronics. 1:26-31. F. '72. Nuclear radiation: insidious
  polluter. F. H. Belt.
Population Bulletin. 26:2-18. N. '70. The first national congress
  on optimum population and the environment [Chicago, June
  7-11, 1970].
Public Relations Journal. 27:6-9. Ap. '71. Earth day—revisited: environment still a major problem, but activists are more mod-
  erate in seeking solutions. Kerryn King.
Ramparts. 9:17-18. Mr. '71. Cleaning of America (don't hold your
  breath). James Ridgeway.
Ramparts. 10:18+. F. '72. Clean water: Nixon vetoes Nixon. James
  Ridgeway.
Reader's Digest. 98:175-80. Ja. '71. Battle tactics for conservation-
  ists. J. N. Miller.
Reader's Digest. 98:31-2+. My. '71. Law that could clean up our
  rivers; Federal refuse act of 1899. J. N. Miller.
Reader's Digest. 99:129-32. N. '71. Needed: an about-face for the
  Corps of engineers. H. S. Reuss.
Reader's Digest. 100:85-9. Mr. '72. How best to protect the environ-
  ment. P. F. Drucker.
Redbook. 137:56-7+. Jl. '71. What you can do now to fight pollu-
  tion. Alice Lake.
Saturday Review. 54:47-8. Je. 5, '71. Skeleton in the garage; mem-
  orandum: Economics of clean air. John Lear.
Saturday Review. 54:20+. Je. 12, '71. Senator Muskie's foreign
  pollution policy; address to UN symposium, May 21, 1971.
  John Lear.
Saturday Review. 54:91. D. 4, '71. Starvation as a policy. P. R.
  Ehrlich and J. P. Holdren.
    Excerpts: Current. 136:61-3. Ja. '72 Ecology of war
Saturday Review. 55:40. Ap. 15, '72. Only one earth; excerpt from
  Action Plan drawn up under guidance of Maurice Strong,
  an Under-secretary General of the UN to be considered at
  the Stockholm conference in June 1972.
Science. 170:945-52. N. 27, '70. American institutions and ecological
  ideals; adaptation of address, December 29, 1969. Leo Marx.
    Discussion. Science. 171:1095-6. Mr. 19, '71.

Science. 171:43-7. Ja. 8, '71. Herbicides in Vietnam: AAAS [American Association for the Advancement of Science] study finds widespread devastation. P. M. Boffey.

Science. 171:385-7. Ja. 29, '71. Paradox of enrichment: destabilization of exploitation ecosystems in ecological time. M. L. Rosenzweig.

Science. 171:659. F. 19, '71. Nixon offers large, mixed bag on environment. Constance Holden.

Science. 172:517. My. 7, '71. Changing attitudes toward environmental problems. P. H. Abelson.

Science. 172:1307-14. Je. 25, '71. International environmental problems: a taxonomy. C. S. Russell and H. H. Landsberg.

Science. 173:38. Jl. 2, '71. DDT stopped, suit dropped; discharge of DDT from Montrose. E. P. Jones.

Science. 174:662-5. N. 12, '71. Sanity in research and evaluation of environmental health. H. E. Stokinger.
        Discussion. Science. 175:835-7. F. 25, '72.

Science. 175:45-6. Ja. 7, '72. Pollution: military's cleanup stresses plumbing, not R&D. Deborah Shapley.

Science. 175:46-8. Ja. 7, '72. Ecosystem analysis: biome approach to environmental research. A. L. Hammond.

*Science. 175:394-5. Ja. 28, '72. Environmental action organizations are suffering from money shortages, slump in public commitment. Constance Holden.

Science. 176:30-3. Ap. 7, '72. National environmental policy act: signs of backlash are evident. Robert Gillette.

Science. 176:146-50. Ap. 14, '72. National environmental policy act: how well is it working? Robert Gillette.

Science Digest. 69:53. Je. '71. Soviets tackle ecology problems.

Science Digest. 71:73-8. Ja. '72. Can land be developed without wrecking nature? W. B. Hartley and Ellen Hartley.

Science News. 99:96. F. 6, '71. Meaningful boost [air pollution standards].

Science News. 99:177-8. Mr. 13, '71. Clean air: an R&D gap.
        Reply. Science News. 99:276. Ap. 24, '71. Emission control R&D. F. W. Bowditch.

Science News. 99:280. Ap. 24, '71. Autos, emission reports and the public.

Science News. 99:280. Ap. 24, '71. Mercury in the air.

Science News. 101:100-1. F. 12, '72. Ecology, survival and society; British manifesto: Blueprint for survival.

Science News. 101:230. Ap. 8, '72. Clean water bills now go to conference committee.

Scientific American. 224:12, 32-42. Ja. '71. Global circulation of atmospheric pollutants. R. E. Newell.

Scientific American. 224:44. F. '71. Defoliation in Chicago; AAAS
    [American Association for the Advancement of Science] report
    on military use of defoliants in Vietnam.
Senior Scholastic. 98:9. Mr. 29, '71. Pollution doesn't stop at the
    border.
Senior Scholastic. 98:3-5. Ap. 26, '71. Where the action is: what
    young people have done [with discussion].
Senior Scholastic. 98:9-10. My. 10, '71. Spaceship Earth revisited.
Seventeen. 30:128-9+. Ap. '71. 5 who fight pollution. Charles
    Remsberg and Bonnie Remsberg.
Society. 9:59-61. F. '72. Environmental celebration. W. B. Devall.
Sports Illustrated. 34:30-2+. Ap. 26, '71. When a law fights a law:
    mining law of 1872 vs Environmental act. Bil Gilbert.
Successful Farming. 70 no4:E 16. Mr. '72. Pesticides in soil: but
    never applied.
Time. 97:84. Ap. 5, '71. Ecology at the supermarket; measures
    taken at Alexander's stores in Los Angeles.
Time. 97:59. Ap. 26, '71. Nader on water.
Time. 97:46. My. 17, '71. Blueprint for breathing; 1970 Clean air
    act.
Time. 97:82. My. 31, '71. What the pollution fight will cost business.
Time. 98:41. Jl. 26, '71. To swim or not to swim.
Time. 98:79. N. 1, '71. Price of progress; conclusions of Barry
    Commoner.
Time. 99:46. Ja. 31, '72. Cheerful sabotage; antipollution tactics.
Time. 99:47. F. 21, '72. Nixon's third round.
Time. 99:44. Mr. 13, '72. Test on taconite; dumping of mine waste
    in Lake Superior.
Today's Health. 49:41-3+. Ap. '71. Bounty hunter wore sneakers.
    Mike Michaelson.

U.S. News & World Report. 69:54-8. N. 23, '70. How to stop pollu-
    tion: interview with Russell Train, White House adviser on
    the environment.
U.S. News & World Report. 70:70-5. Mr. 29, '71. Coming Govern-
    ment moves in war against pollution; interview. W. D. Ruckels-
    haus.
U.S. News & World Report. 71:60-2. N. 22, '71. Pollution and in-
    dustry: pros, cons of growing fight.
U.S. News & World Report. 71:68-9. D. 6, '71. Drive to find jobs
    for victims of pollution war.
U.S. News & World Report. 72:36-7. F. 21, '72. Tougher drive to
    clean up air, water.
U.S. News & World Report. 72:92-3. Ap. 10, '72. Crusade for clean
    earth runs into trouble.

U.S. News & World Report. 72:52. Ap. 24, '72. Under way: drive to clean up the lakes.

UNESCO Courier. 24:4-32. Jl. '71. S.O.S. environment; symposium.

UNESCO Courier. 24:38-43. Ag. '71. Mind extinct? Unesco's work. Wayne McEwing.

UNESCO Courier. 25:4-8+. F. '72. In defense of DDT and other pesticides; excerpts from address, November 8, 1971. N. E. Borlaug.

University of Toronto Law Journal. 21 no 2:173-251. '71. The international legal aspects of pollution; symposium.

Vantage. 22:[3-7]. My/Je. '71. The UN's role in the preservation of the human environment. Barbara Ward.

Vital Speeches of the Day. 37:410-13. Ap. 15, '71. Engineering education; ecological issues; address, February 2, 1971. Myron Tribus.

Vital Speeches of the Day. 37:492-4. Je. 1, '71. Science and technology; address, April 30, 1971. A. H. Aymond.

Vital Speeches of the Day. 37:509-12. Je. 1, '71. Economy & environment; the need for integrity; address, April 28, 1971. Lowry Wyatt.

Vital Speeches of the Day. 38:86-90. N. 15, '71. Right on, Establishment; address, October 11, 1971. M. J. Caserio.

Vital Speeches of the Day. 38:290-3. Mr. 1, '72. Zero discharge; aims of the Muskie bill; address, January 6, 1972. J. T. Connor.

Vital Speeches of the Day. 38:304-6. Mr. 1, '72. Pesticides and public opinion; address, January 12, 1972. H. L. Straube.

Vital Speeches of the Day. 38:337-40. Mr. 15, '72. Healthy economy and a healthy environment; address, February 22, 1972. J. H. Evans.

*Vital Speeches of the Day. 38:381-4. Ap. 1, '72. Question of ecology: the cries of wolf; address, December 14, 1971. A. L. Jones.

Wall Street Journal. p 14. S. 23, '70. Meet a prime polluter: Uncle Sam. Dennis Farney.

Wall Street Journal. p 1+. O. 27, '70. Saving the scenery: new Federal programs may strengthen effort to guard environment. Burt Schorr.

Wall Street Journal. p 16. Ap. 13, '71. Ecological shootout at Black Mesa. W. E. Blundell.

Wall Street Journal. p 14. Ap. 19, '71. Labor's pollution campaign goes up in smoke. Norman Pearlstine.

Washington Monthly. 2:13-20. S. '70. Congress and pollution: the gentleman's agreement. Douglas Ross and Harold Wolman.

Weekly Compilation of Presidential Documents. 7:187-204. F. 15, '71. The President's 1971 environmental program: the President's message to the Congress outlining his program.

> *Excerpts.* Department of State Bulletin. 64:253-6. Mr. 1, '71. International aspects of the 1971 environmental program; U.S. News & World Report. 70:72-7. F. 22, '71. Billions to fight pollution.

WHO Chronicle. 25:25-8. Ja. '71. From sanitary engineering to environmental health: engineering education faces the future.

World Petroleum. 41:30-1. Ag. '70. War on pollution is USA political issue: one very large problem resulting from the public concern over ecology is the increasing conflict between the environmental crisis and the nation's growing crisis in energy and energy sources. Clyde La Motte.

Yachting. 129:70+. Je. '71. Pollution and policing; Lake George patrol. Mel Crook.

Yachting. 130:56-7+. Jl. '71. Ecology crisis, what you can do. Ben Emory.

> *Editorial comment.* Yachting. 130:33. Jl. '71. Challenge.